PENGUIN BOOKS — GREAT FOOD

Murder in the Kitchen

ALICE B. TOKLAS (1877–1967) was born in San Francisco, California. Long before Julia Child discovered French cooking, Toklas was sampling local dishes and collecting recipes in Paris between the wars. She was confidante, lover, cook, secretary, muse, editor and critic to the writer Gertrude Stein. Together they hosted a salon that attracted many influential writers and artists of the day, including Ernest Hemingway, Paul Bowles, F. Scott Fitzgerald, Picasso and Matisse. First published in 1954, *The Alice B. Toklas Cookbook* is a rich mixture of cookery, anecdote and reminiscence, evoking 1950s Paris and meals shared with famous friends. It is one of the bestselling cookbooks of all time.

Murder in the Kitchen

ALICE B. TOKLAS

PENGUIN BOOKS

PENGUIN BOOKS

Published by the Penguin Group
Penguin Books Ltd, 80 Strand, London WC2R 0RL, England
Penguin Group (USA) Inc., 375 Hudson Street, New York, New York 10014, USA
Penguin Group (Canada), 90 Eglinton Avenue East, Suite 700, Toronto, Ontario,
Canada M4P 2Y3 (a division of Pearson Penguin Canada Inc.)
Penguin Ireland, 25 St Stephen's Green, Dublin 2, Ireland
(a division of Penguin Books Ltd)
Penguin Group (Australia), 250 Camberwell Road, Camberwell, Victoria 3124,
Australia (a division of Pearson Australia Group Pty Ltd)
Penguin Books India Pvt Ltd, 11 Community Centre,
Panchsheel Park, New Delhi – 110 017, India
Penguin Group (NZ), 67 Apollo Drive, Rosedale, Auckland 0632, New Zealand
(a division of Pearson New Zealand Ltd)
Penguin Books (South Africa) (Pty) Ltd, 24 Sturdee Avenue,
Rosebank, Johannesburg 2196, South Africa

Penguin Books Ltd, Registered Offices: 80 Strand, London WC2R 0RL, England

www.penguin.com

The Alice B. Toklas Cookbook first published 1954
This extract published in Penguin Books 2011

3

Copyright 1954 by the Estate of Alice B. Toklas
All rights reserved

Set in 10.75/13 pt Berkeley Oldstyle Book
Typeset by Jouve (UK), Milton Keynes
Printed in Great Britain by Clays Ltd, St Ives plc

Cover design based on a pattern for an eighteenth-century dish. Tin-glazed
earthernware with blue paint. (Photograph copyright © Victora & Albert Museum.)
Picture Research by Samantha Johnson. Lettering by Stephen Raw

ISBN: 978-0-241-95103-3

www.greenpenguin.co.uk

MIX
Paper from
responsible sources
FSC™ C018179

Penguin Books is committed to a sustainable
future for our business, our readers and our
planet. This book is made from paper certified
by the Forest Stewardship Council.

Contents

Dishes for Artists

Before coming to Paris I was interested in food but not in doing any cooking. When in 1908 I went to live with Gertrude Stein at the rue de Fleurus she said we would have American food for Sunday-evening supper, she had had enough French and Italian cooking; the servant would be out and I should have the kitchen to myself. So I commenced to cook the simple dishes I had eaten in the homes of the San Joaquin Valley in California – fricasseed chicken, corn bread, apple and lemon pie. Then when the pie crust received Gertrude Stein's critical approval I made mince-meat and at Thanksgiving we had a turkey that Hélène the cook roasted but for which I prepared the dressing. Gertrude Stein not being able to decide whether she preferred mushrooms, chestnuts, or oysters in the dressing, all three were included. The experiment was successful and frequently repeated; it gradually entered into my repertoire, which expanded as I grew experimental and adventurous.

BASS FOR PICASSO

One day when Picasso was to lunch with us I decorated a fish in a way that I thought would amuse him. I chose a fine striped bass and cooked it according to a theory of my grandmother who had no experience in cooking and who rarely saw her kitchen but who had endless theories about cooking as well as about many other things. She contended that a fish having lived its life in water, once caught, should have no further contact with the element in which it had been born and raised. She recommended that it be roasted or poached in wine or cream or butter. So I made a *court-bouillon* of dry white wine with whole peppers, salt, a laurel leaf,* a sprig of thyme, a blade of mace, an onion with a clove stuck in it, a carrot, a leek, and a bouquet of *fines herbes*. This was gently boiled in the fish-kettle for ½ hour and then put aside to cool. Then the fish was placed on the rack, the fish-kettle covered and slowly brought to a boil, and the fish poached for 20 minutes. Taken from the fire it was left to cool in the *court-bouillon*. It was then carefully drained, dried, and placed on the fish platter. A short time before serving it I covered the fish with an ordinary mayonnaise and, using a pastry trube, decorated it with a red mayonnaise, not coloured with catsup – horror of horrors – but with tomato paste. Then I made a design with sieved hard-boiled eggs, the whites and the yolks apart, with truffles and with finely chopped *fines herbes*. I was proud of my *chef d'œuvre* when it was served and Picasso exclaimed at its beauty. But, said he, should it not rather have been made in honour of Matisse than of me.

Picasso was for many years on a strict diet; in fact he managed somehow to continue it through the World

* The leaf must come from Apollo's Laurel (*Laurus Nobilis*), better known outside France as the bay.

War and the Occupation and, characteristically, only relaxed after the Liberation. Red meat was proscribed but that presented no difficulties for in those days beef was rarely served by the French except the inevitable roast fillet of beef with *sauce Madère*. Chicken too was not well considered, though a roast leg of mutton was viewed with more favour. Or we would have a tender loin of veal preceded by a spinach *soufflé*, spinach having been highly recommended by Picasso's doctor and a *soufflé* being the least objectionable way of preparing it. Could it not be made more interesting by adding a sauce. But what sauce would Picasso's diet permit. I would give him a choice. The *soufflé* would be cooked in a well-buttered mould, placed in boiling water, and when sufficiently cooked turned into a hollow dish around which in equal divisions would be placed a Hollandaise sauce, a cream sauce, and a tomato sauce. It was my hope that the tri-coloured sauces would make the spinach *soufflé* look less nourishing. Cruel enigma, said Picasso, when the *soufflé* was served to him.

The only painter who ever gave me a recipe was Francis Picabia and though it is only a dish of eggs it merits the name of its creator.

ŒUFS FRANCIS PICABIA

Break 8 eggs into a bowl and mix them well with a fork, add salt but no pepper. Pour them into a saucepan – yes, a saucepan, no, not a frying pan. Put the saucepan over a very, very low flame, keep turning them with a fork while very slowly adding in very small quantities ½ lb.

butter – not a speck less, rather more if you can bring yourself to it. It should take ½ hour to prepare this dish. The eggs of course are not scrambled but with the butter, no substitute admitted, produce a suave consistency that perhaps only *gourments* will appreciate.

When the Germans in 1940 were advancing we were at Bilignin and had no precise information concerning their progress through France. Could one believe the radio. We didn't. We heard cannon-fire. Then it grew louder. The next morning dressing at the window I saw German planes firing on French planes, not more than two miles away. This decided me to act in the way any forethoughtful housekeeper should. We would take the car into Belley and make provision for any eventuality as I had done that April morning of 1906 when the fire in San Francisco had broken out after the earthquake. Then I had been able to secure two hams and my father had brought back four hundred cigarettes. With these one might, he said, not only exist but be able to be hospitable. So at Belley we bought two hams and hundreds of cigarettes and some groceries – the garden at Bilignin would provide fruit and vegetables. The main road was filled with refugees, just as it had been in 1914 and in 1917. Everything that was happening had already been experienced, like a half-awakening from nightmare. The firing grew louder and then the first armoured car flew past. Crushed, we took the little dust road back to Bilignin. The widow Roux, who for many summers had been our devoted servant and later during the Occupation proved to be our loyal friend, opened the big iron gates to let the car through and we unloaded the provisions. What were we to do with the two enormous uncooked hams. In what could we cook them and in what way so that they would keep indefinitely. We decided upon *Eau-de-Vie de Marc* for which the Bugey is well known. It seemed madly extravagant but we lived on those two hams during the long lean winter that followed and well into the following spring, and the *Eau-de-Vie de Marc* in which they were cooked, carefully bottled and corked, toned up winter vegetables. We threw nothing, but absolutely nothing away, living through a war in an occupied country.

The Baronne Pierlot, our neighbour, was *châtelaine* at Beon, some ten miles away. One day, before the war, we had driven over to a *gouter** to which she had bidden us. It was being served in the summer dining-room whose windows and door gave on to a vast terrace. In the foreground was the marsh of the Rhône Valley lately reclaimed by the planting of Lombardy poplars, to the south the mountains of the Grande Chartreuse, to the left in the distance the French Alps, and over it all the Tiepolo blue sky. The table in the dining-room set for twenty or more was elaborately decorated with pink roses. Madame Pierlot's observant eye passed quickly and lightly over each object on the table. I heard her tell the *valet-de-chambre* to ask the cook for the *pièce de résistance* and to place it in the empty space waiting for it in the centre of the table. But Marc did not leave the room, he merely took a cake from the serving table and

* Here, a lavish afternoon tea-party.

5

put it in the empty space. There was evidently some *con-tretemps.* I was enlightened when I caught knowing looks passing between Gertrude Stein and one of the daughters-in-law of the house. It was Gertrude Stein's white poodle, a very neat thief, who had done away with whatever had been in the centre of the table. Later when Madame Pierlot, to show that she had forgiven the dog, threw him a piece of cake we could not protest that it was against our principles to reward a misdeed.

Madame Pierlot was an old friend of Paul Claudel and there had been a long controversial correspondence over the years, largely on religious subjects; Claudel a devout Catholic, Madame Pierlot not. Bernard Fay said that she had been converted once and forever by Jean-Jacques Rousseau. She told Gertrude Stein one day that Claudel's letters were beginning to bore her and she was equally bored by having to answer him. She had written to him saying that they would no longer defend their opinions, that they would no longer write to each other, but they would remain the same good old friends they had always been. Claudel could not resist having the last word. He wrote that in spite of her continuously avowed unbelief he was certain that when he died he would find her in Heaven welcoming him with arms extended, to which she replied – Who tells you that I am to die before you.

If Madame Pierlot was known as an exquisite hostess it was not only for her wit and charm or for her impeccable taste in choosing her guests and her menus, but also for the care with which her old cook, Perrine, prepared the menus. Madame Pierlot told me that when she was engaging her to come to be her cook she asked her if she knew how to prepare several complicated dishes which she mentioned. She saw that Perrine had had a large experience. As she was well recommended, I decided, Madame Pierlot told me, to engage her, but I told her that it was on the condition that she would forget everything she knew and follow the recipes and the instructions I would give her.

Our enchanting old friend was as original in her housekeeping as in everything else. Long ago the *Figaro* which was then the newspaper read by the fashionable world asked well-known society women to contribute recipes which were to be printed in a special column. When Madame Pierlot was asked to be one of the contributors she sent the recipe for

GIGOT DE LA CLINIQUE

A surgeon living in the provinces, as fond of good cheer as he was learned, invented this recipe which we acquired by bribing his cook. No leg of venison can compare with a simple leg of mutton prepared in the following manner. Eight days in advance you will cover the leg of mutton with the marinade called Baume Samaritain, composed of wine – old Burgundy, Beaune, or Chambertin – and virgin olive oil. Into this balm to which you have already added the usual condiments of salt, pepper, bay leaf, thyme, beside an atom of ginger root, put a pinch of cayenne, a nutmeg cut into small pieces, a handful of crushed juniper berries, and lastly a dessertspoon of powdered sugar (effective as musk in perfumery) which serves to fix the different aromas.

Twice a day you will turn the *gigot*. Now we come to the main point of the preparation. After you have placed the *gigot* in the marinade you will arm yourself with a surgical syringe of a size to hold ½ pint which you will fill with ½ cup of cognac and ½ cup of fresh orange juice. Inject the contents of the syringe into the fleshy part of the *gigot* in three different spots. Refill the syringe with the same contents and inject into the *gigot* twice more. Each day you will fill the syringe with the marinade and inject the contents into the *gigot*. At the end of the week the leg of mutton is ready to be roasted; perfumed with the condiments and the spices, completely permeated by the various flavours, it has been transfused into a strange and exquisite venison. Roast and serve with the usual venison sauce to which has been added just before serving 2 tablespoons of the blood of a hare.*

Everyone thought that the syringe was a whimsy, that Madame Pierlot was making mock of them. Not at all. Years later I found it in that great collection of French recipes, Bertrand Guegan's *Le Grand Cuisinier Français*. The Baronne Pierlot's recipe is classified, it has entered into the *Grande Cuisine Française*.

* A marinade is a bath of wine, herbs, oil, vegetables, vinegars, and so on, in which fish or meat destined for particular dishes repose for specified periods and acquire virtue.

Murder in the Kitchen

Cook books have always intrigued and seduced me. When I was still a dilettante in the kitchen they held my attention, even the dull ones, from cover to cover, the way crime and murder stories did Gertrude Stein.

When we first began reading Dashiell Hammett, Gertrude Stein remarked that it was his modern note to have disposed of his victims before the story commenced. Goodness knows how many were required to follow as the result of the first crime. And so it is in the kitchen. Murder and sudden death seem as unnatural there as they should be anywhere else. They can't, they can never become acceptable facts. Food is far too pleasant to combine with horror. All the same, facts, even distasteful facts, must be accepted and we shall see how, before any story of cooking begins, crime is inevitable. That is why cooking is not an entirely agreeable pastime. There is too much that must happen in advance of the actual cooking. This doesn't of course apply to food that emerges stainless from deep freeze. But the marketing and cooking I know are French and it was in France, where freezing units are unknown, that in due course I graduated at the stove.

In earlier days, memories of which are scattered among my chapters, if indulgent friends on this or that Sunday evening or party occasion said that the cooking

I produced wasn't bad, it neither beguiled nor flattered me into liking or wanting to do it. The only way to learn to cook is to cook, and for me, as for so many others, it suddenly and unexpectedly became a disagreeable necessity to have to do it when war came and Occupation followed. It was in those conditions of rationing and shortage that I learned not only to cook seriously but to buy food in a restricted market and not to take too much time in doing it, since there were so many more important and more amusing things to do. It was at this time, then, that murder in the kitchen began.

The first victim was a lively carp brought to the kitchen in a covered basket from which nothing could escape. The fish man who sold me the carp said he had no time to kill, scale, or clean it, nor would he tell me with which of these horrible necessities one began. It wasn't difficult to know which was the most repellent. So quickly to the murder and have it over with. On the docks of Puget Sound I had seen fishermen grasp the tail of a huge salmon and lifting it high bring it down on the dock with enough force to kill it. Obviously I was not a fisherman nor was the kitchen table a dock. Should I not dispatch my first victim with a blow on the head from a heavy mallet? After an appraising glance at the lively fish it was evident he would escape attempts aimed at his head. A heavy sharp knife came to my mind as the classic, the perfect choice, so grasping, with my left hand well covered with a dishcloth, for the teeth might be sharp, the lower jaw of the carp, and the knife in my right, I carefully, deliberately found the base of its vertebral column and plunged the knife in. I let go my grasp and looked to see what had happened. Horror of horrors. The carp was dead, killed, assassinated, murdered in the first, second, and third degree. Limp, I fell into a chair, with my hands still unwashed reached for a cigarette, lighted it, and waited for the police to come and take me into custody. After a second cigarette my courage returned and I went to prepare Mr Carp for the table. I scraped off the scales, cut off the fins, cut open the underside, and emptied out a great deal of what I did not care to look at, thoroughly washed and dried the fish, and put it aside while I prepared

CARP STUFFED WITH CHESTNUTS

For a 3-lb. carp, chop a medium-sized onion and cook it gently in 3 tablespoons butter. Add a 2-inch slice of bread cut into small cubes which have previously been soaked in dry, white wine and squeezed dry, 1 tablespoon chopped parsley, 2 chopped shallots, 1 clove of pressed garlic, 1 teaspoon salt, ¼ teaspoon freshly ground pepper, ¼ teaspoon powdered mace, the same of laurel (bay) and of thyme, and 12 boiled and peeled chestnuts. Mix well, allow to cool, add 1 raw egg, stuff the cavity and head of the fish, carefully snare with skewers, tie the head so that nothing will escape in cooking. Put aside for at least a couple of hours. Put 2 cups dry white wine into an earthenware dish, place the fish in the dish, salt to taste. Cook in the oven for 20 minutes at 375°. Baste, and cover the fish with a thick coating of very fine cracker crumbs, dot with 3 tablespoons melted butter, and cook for 20 minutes more. Serve very hot accompanied by noodles. Serves 4. The head of a carp is enormous. Many continentals consider it the most delectable morsel.

NOODLES

Sift 2 cups flour, 1 teaspoon salt, and a pinch of nutmeg, add the yolks of 5 eggs and 1 whole egg. Mix thoroughly with a fork and then knead on a floured board, form into a ball, wrap in a cloth, and put aside for several hours. Divide into three parts. Roll each one in turn on a lightly floured board to tissue-paper thinness. Dry for ½ hour, roll up, and cut into strips ¼ inch wide. Bring 1 quart water with 1 teaspoon salt to a hard boil. Place noodles a few at a time into boiling water, stir gently with a fork, reduce heat, and boil slowly for 10 minutes. Drain off all the water and add 3 tablespoons melted butter. These noodles are very delicate. Serves 4.

It was in the market of Palma de Mallorca that our French cook tried to teach me to murder by smothering. There is no reason why this crime should have been committed publicly or that I should have been expected to participate. Jeanne was just showing off. When the crowd of market women who had gathered about her began screaming and gesticulating, I retreated. When we met later to drive back in the carry-all filled with our marketing to Terreno where we had a villa I refused to sympathize with Jeanne. She said the Mallorcans were bloodthirsty, didn't they go to bullfights and pay an advanced price for the meat of the beasts they had seen killed in the ring, didn't they prefer to chop off the heads of innocent pigeons instead of humanely smothering them which was the way to prevent all fowl from bleeding to death and so make them fuller and tastier. Had she not tried to explain this to them, to teach them, to show them how an intelligent humane person went about killing pigeons, but no they didn't want to learn, they preferred their own brutal ways. At lunch when she served the pigeons Jeanne discreetly said nothing. Discussing food which she enjoyed above everything had been discouraged at table. But her fine black eyes were eloquent. If the small-sized pigeons the island produced had not achieved jumbo size, squabs they unquestionably were, and larger and more succulent squabs than those we had eaten at the excellent restaurant at Palma.

Later we went back to Paris and then there was war and after a lifetime there was peace. One day passing the *concierge's loge* he called me and said he had something someone had left for us. He said he would bring it to me, which he did and which I wished he hadn't when I saw what it was, a crate of six white pigeons and a note from a friend saying she had nothing better to offer us from her home in the country, ending with, But as Alice is clever she will make something delicious of them. It is certainly a mistake to allow a reputation for cleverness to be born and spread by loving friends. It is so cheaply acquired and so dearly paid for. Six white pigeons to be smothered, to be plucked, to be cleaned, and all this to be accomplished before Gertrude Stein returned for she didn't like to see work being done. If only I had the courage the two hours before her return would easily

13

suffice. A large cup of strong black coffee would help. This was before a lovely Brazilian told me that in her country a large cup of black coffee was always served before going to bed to ensure a good night's rest. Not yet having acquired this knowledge the black coffee made me lively and courageous. I carefully found the spot on poor innocent Dove's throat where I was to press and pressed. The realization had never come to me before that one saw with one's fingertips as well as one's eyes. It was a most unpleasant experience, though as I laid out one by one the sweet young corpses there was no denying one could become accustomed to murdering. So I plucked the pigeons, emptied them, and was ready to cook

BRAISED PIGEONS ON CROÛTONS

For 6 pigeons cut ½ lb. salt pork in small cubes, place in Dutch oven with 6 tablespoons butter, place pigeons in oven, brown slightly, cover and cook over low flame for 1 hour turning and basting frequently. While pigeons are cooking wash and carefully dry 2 lb. mushrooms. Chop them very fine, and pass through a coarse sieve, cook over brisk fire in ¼ lb. butter until liquid has evaporated. Reduce flame and add 1 cup heavy cream sauce and ½ cup heavy cream. Spread on 6 one-half-inch slices of bread that have been lightly browned in butter. Spread the *purée* of mushrooms on the *croûtons*. Place the pigeons on the *croûtons*. Skim the fat from the juice in the Dutch oven, add 2 tablespoons Madeira, bring to a boil, and pour over pigeons. Salt for this dish depends upon how salty the pork is. Serves 6 to 12 according to size of pigeons.

The next murder was not of my doing. During six months which we spent in the country we raised Barbary ducks. They are larger than ordinary ducks and are famous for the size of their livers. They do not quack and are not friendly. Down in the Ain everyone shoots. Many of the farmers go off to work in the fields with a gun slung over a shoulder and not infrequently return with a bird or two. Occasionally a farmer would sell us a pheasant or a partridge. An English friend staying with us, astonished to find farmers shooting, remarked, When everyone shoots no one shoots. Our nearest neighbour had a so-called bird dog, mongrel she certainly was, ruby coat like an Irish setter but her head was flat, her paws too large, her tail too short. We would see Diane on the road, she was not sympathetic. The large iron portals at Bilignin were sometimes left open when Gertrude Stein took the car out for a short while, and one morning Diane, finding them open, came into the court and saw the last of our Barbary ducks, Blanchette, because she was blue-black. Perhaps innocently perhaps not, opinion was divided later, she began to chase Blanchette. She would come running at the poor bewildered duck from a distance, charge upon her, retreat, and recommence. The cook, having seen from the kitchen window what was happening, hastened out. The poor duck was on her back and Diane was madly barking and running about. By the time I got to the court the cook was tenderly carrying a limp Blanchette in her arms to the kitchen. Having chased Diane out of the court, I closed the portals and returned to my work in the vegetable garden supposing the episode to be over. Not at all. Presently the cook appeared, her face whiter than her apron. Madame, she said, poor Blanchette is no more. That wretched dog frightened her to death. Her heart was beating so furiously I saw there was but one thing to do. I gave her three tablespoonfuls of *eau-de-vie*, that will give her a good flavour. And then I killed her. How does Madame wish her to be cooked. Surprised at the turn the affair had taken, I answered feebly, With orange sauce.

There was considerable talk in the hamlet. While we were walking along the road someone would say, What a pity, or Your beautiful bird! to which we would answer that we would have had to be eating her soon anyway. But Diane's master did not know what attitude to take until I sent his wife a basket of globe egg plants, almost white and yellow tomatoes, and a few gumbos (okra), none of which she had seen before. Then he came to thank us for his wife and presented a large pot of fresh butter she had sent us. He knew our cook felt that his dog had caused the death of our duck. We wiped out the memory of the misadventure in thanking each other for the gifts. So Blanchette was cooked as

DUCK WITH ORANGE SAUCE

Put the bird aside and cook the rest of the giblets including the neck in 2 cups water with 1 teaspoon salt, ¼ teaspoon pepper, 1 small onion with a clove stuck in it, a shallot, ½ laurel leaf, a sprig of thyme, and a small blade of mace. Cover and cook slowly. When the juice has reduced to 1 cup put aside. Cut 1 peeled orange into half a dozen pieces and put inside the duck. Cut the orange peel into small pieces and boil covered in ½ cup water for 10 minutes. Roast the duck in a 400° oven in a pan with 3 tablespoons butter for ½ hour, basting and turning the duck three times. Put the orange peel and the liver in a mortar. Moisten with ⅓ cup of the best white curaçao and crush to an even paste. Add to this the cup of giblet juice and the juice in the pan from which the fat has been skimmed. Heat thoroughly but do not allow to boil, strain and serve in preheated metal sauce boat. Place very thinly sliced unpeeled oranges on the duck and serve. Sufficient for 4.

Many times I held the thought to kill a stupid or obstinate cook, but as long as the thought was held murder was not committed. Then a gay and enchanting Austrian came to cook for me. He was a perfect cook. Quietly and expeditiously Kaspar, as I shall call him, prepared the most intricate and complicated dishes for us, nothing was too much trouble for him to undertake. He would make us ice cream in individual moulds in the form of eggs on a nest of coloured spun sugar. He delighted in making cakes that represented objects appropriate to each person, a book for Gertrude Stein, a rose for Sir Francis Rose, a peacock for a very vain young lady, and a little dog for me. He used to receive the visits of an extremely pretty young girl, Lili, who looked as if she had stepped out of an Offenbach opera. Gertrude Stein and I were delighted with them. At Christmas we asked them to accept amongst their gifts a supper with champagne at the restaurant of their choice for the traditional *réveillon*. Gradually Kaspar began to confide in me. Life was not as happy for him as it had been. In the beginning there was only his fiancée Lili, his angel, but now there was a second, a devil, who wanted him to marry her and who was threatening to kill him if he didn't. And he told us that he and Hitler had been born in the same village and that anyone in the village was like all the others and that they were all a little strange. This was in 1936 and we already knew Hitler was very strange indeed. Kaspar was perhaps not so much strange as weak, loving wine, women, and song. But he continued to be a perfect cook. He had been for several years a cook at Frau Sacher's restaurant and frequently baked us the well-known

SACHER TORTE

Cream ½ cup butter, gradually add 1 cup sugar, the grated peel of 1 lemon, 4 oz. melted chocolate, the yolks of 6 eggs, fold in the beaten whites of 6 eggs, and 3 tablespoons flour. Butter and flour a flat cake pan and bake for 40 minutes in a 325° oven. Let cool in pan. When perfectly cold, cut in half and spread the following mixture between the two layers.

2 oz. chocolate melted, to which add 1 teaspoon powdered coffee dissolved in ½ cup hot water. When perfectly smooth beat in 2 yolks of eggs. Beat 1 cup .

heavy cream sweetened with 3 tablespoons icing sugar. Add first mixture to the whipped cream.

Cover the cake with apricot jelly or strained apricot jam and ice with chocolate icing.

Kaspar also liked to serve

LINZER TORTE

½ cup powdered almonds, 1 cup flour, ½ cup butter, ½ cup sugar, the yolks of 2 boiled eggs sieved, a pinch of cinnamon, a pinch of nutmeg, grated peel of ½ lemon. Cut the butter and flour with knives or pastry blender, add the other ingredients in the above order, finally add 3 teaspoons rum. Put aside in the refrigerator for a couple of hours. Roll out three-quarters of the dough and fit into buttered pie plate with detachable bottom, fill with raspberry jam. Roll out rest of dough, cut with pastry wheel into strips ½ in. wide and place on pie in lattices. Paint lightly with beaten egg. Bake in 350° oven for ½ hour.

Here is the last dish Kaspar served us.

GYPSY GOULASH

1½ lb. fillet of beef in slices of ¼ inch thickness, cut in lenghts of ¼ inch width, browned in lard with 1 teaspoon salt, 1 tablespoon paprika, and 1 tablespoon flour, 4 large onions sliced, ¾ lb. potatoes sliced. When lightly browned add 2 cups red wine, 1 cup sour cream, and enough *bouillon* to cover. Put in covered casserole in 375° oven for 1 hour. Add ½ cup sour cream before serving. Serve with noodles. Serves 4.

One afternoon as Gertrude Stein and I were coming home someone came out of our door and passed in the court. She had small snappy dark eyes. The devil, Gertrude Stein inquired. Presumably, I answered. The glimpse I had of her left me uneasy for Kaspar. We wanted him to be happy and to stay with us as our servant. Later I went into the kitchen to see him. He was sitting at the table, his head in his arms. He jumped up when he saw me. What is it, I asked. The devil, Madame, the devil came to see me with a bottle of precious Tokay as a gift. The devil wanted to poison me, to kill me. The fiend poured a glass and passed it to me. Just as I was about to toast her I noticed that she had poured none for herself, her glass was empty, and that she had not taken out the cork with a corkscrew. She was going to poison me. I threw the bottle at her. I shoved her about. I threw her out. Oh Madame, the devil will get me yet or she will kill me. I sent him off to his room.

The next morning there was no Kaspar in the kitchen. Towards noon I asked the *concierge* to go up to his room to see what had happened. He returned to report that the door was open, the room empty except for a strapped trunk. He had not seen Kaspar all morning but the dark lady had been there about two hours ago. What could we do. Nothing but wait for Lili to turn up which she did late in the afternoon. As pretty, dainty, and as elegant as usual but her eyes red and swollen. She had

had a wire from Kaspar as long as a letter which proved, she said, how distraught he was. He had gone off with the devil, useless to hunt for them, they were leaving Paris. He would always love his angel but their happiness together was over forever. She should go to tell this to the good ladies, they would pay her what they owed him, for three weeks and six days, and with this she should buy herself a *frivolité* as a last souvenir of her adoring Kaspar.

While I was reading this Lili was gently sobbing into a delicate white handkerchief. I led her into the big room and left her with Gertrude Stein while I prepared tea. She came running when she saw the tray with three cups. But she put her handkerchief away and quietly drank several cups of tea and ate the last of Kaspar's perfect Viennese pastry that we were to taste. What are you going to do, we asked Lili. Go on with my work with the good kind Princess, she will understand. When my eyes are no longer red and I shall have forgotten sweet weak Kaspar life will begin again. Then I paid her her faithless lover's wages. She thanked me and counted the bills. With a sob and a sigh she neatly folded and put them in her handbag. Let us hear from you, I said as she left.

But for months we didn't, then we received wedding announcements. In France this is done by the bride's family to the left, by the groom's family to the right. Lili's family way off in an unpronounceable village in Austria had the honour and so on and then the groom's family, two grandmother's and a grandfather, his parents, his brothers, his sisters, all sprinkled with military medals and *Légions d'Honneur* and civil titles, announced that

21

the son was marrying Lili. She had entered a well-established bourgeois family with nothing more to fear.

This is the last souvenir of Kaspar:

A TENDER TART

½ cup and 1 tablespoon butter, 1 cup and 2 tablespoons flour, 1 egg yolk, blend with knives or pastry blender, add only enough water to hold together, knead lightly, put aside in refrigerator. Stir 2 eggs and 1 cup plus 2 tablespoons sugar for 20 minutes. Do not beat. Add 1 teaspoon vanilla and 1 cup finely chopped hazel nuts. Roll out a little more than half the dough, place in deep pie plate with detachable bottom, fill with egg-sugar-nut mixture. Roll out remaining dough and cover tart, press the edges together so that the bottom and top crusts adhere. Bake for ½ hour in 350° oven. Exquisite.

Food to which Aunt Pauline and Lady Godiva Led Us

When in 1916 Gertrude Stein commenced driving Aunt Pauline for the American Fund for French Wounded, she was a responsible if not an experienced driver. She knew how to do everything but go in reverse. She said she would be like the French Army, never have to do such a thing. Delivering to hospitals in Paris and the suburbs offered no difficulties, for there was practically no civilian traffic. One day we were asked to make a delivery to a military hospital in Montereau, where we would lunch after the visit to the hospital. It was late by the time that had been accomplished and the court of the inn that had been recommended was crowded with military cars. When Gertrude Stein proposed leaving Aunt Pauline, for so our delivery truck had been baptized – not in champagne, only in white wine – in the entrance of the court, I protested. It was barring the exit. We can't leave it in the road, she said. That would be too tempting. The large dining-room was filled with officers. The lunch, for wartime, was good. We were waiting for coffee when an officer came to our table and, saluting, said, The truck with a Red Cross in the entrance to the court belongs to you. Oh yes, we proudly said in unison. It is unfortunately barring the exit, he said, so that none of the cars in the court can get out. I am afraid I must ask you to back it out. Oh that, cried Gertrude

Stein, I cannot do, as if it were an unpardonable sin he were asking her to commit. Perhaps, he continued, if you come with me we might together be able to do it. Which they did. But Gertrude Stein was not yet convinced that she would have to learn to go in reverse.

If Aunt Pauline had led us to Montereau on her first adventure, she was soon doing better. The committee of the American Fund had asked us to open a depot for distributing to several departments with headquarters at Perpignan. Aunt Pauline – Model T, bless her – made no more than thirty miles an hour, so we were always late at inns, hotels, and restaurants for meals. But at Saulieu they would serve us for lunch *Panade Veloutée*, Ham Croquettes, and *Pêches Flambées*. They were cooked with delicacy and distinction. I got the recipe for

FLAMING PEACHES

Fresh peaches are preferable, though canned ones can be substituted. If fresh, take 6 and cover with boiling water for a few minutes and peel. Poach in 1½ cups water over low flame for 3 or 4 minutes. Place in a chafing dish, add ¼ cup sugar and ¾ cup peach brandy. Bring to the table and light the chafing dish. When the syrup is about to boil light and ladle it over the peaches. Serve each peach lighted. This is a simple, tasty, and effective dessert.

As we came into the dining-room I had noticed a man wandering about whose appearance disturbed me, he looked suspiciously like a German. German officer prisoners did occasionally escape. When the *maître d'hôtel* received our compliments for the fine cooking, I asked him who the man was and he said he was the proprietor of the hotel and had just been released from Germany where he had been a civilian prisoner. He had been *chef* for a number of years to the Kaiser, which not only accounted for the quality of the food but for the clothes which had misled me.

Aunt Pauline took several days to get us to Lyon where we were to lunch at La Mère Fillioux's famous restaurant. As a centre of gastronomy it was famous for a number of dishes, so La Mère Fillioux's menu was typical of Lyon. It is the habit in Lyon and thereabouts for restaurants and hotels to have set menus called *le diner fin* and *le déjeuner fin*, the choicest dinner and the choicest lunch. We had her choicest lunch, *Lavarets au beurre*,* hearts of artichokes with truffled *foie gras*, steamed capon with *quenelles*, and a *tarte Louise*. Lyon is an excellent marketing centre. Fish served at lunch is caught in the morning, vegetables and fruits are of that morning's picking, which is of first importance in their preparation. Mère Fillioux was a short compact woman in a starched enveloping apron with a short, narrow, but formidable knife which she brandished as she moved from table to table carving each chicken. That was her pleasure and her privilege which she never relinquished to another. She was an expert carver. She placed a fork in the chicken once and for all. Neither she nor the plate moved, the legs and the wings fell, the two breasts, in less than a matter of

---

* Lavarets are fish found in the lakes of Switzerland and the Haute Savoie.

minutes, and she was gone. After the war, she carved a fair-sized turkey for eight of us with the same technique and with as little effort. When the fish appeared at our table she came to it and passed her hand about an inch above our plates to see that they were of the right temperature. Later she returned and with her little knife carved the largest and whitest chicken I ever saw. A whole chicken was always dedicated to each table, even if there was only one person at it. Not to have any small economies gave style to the restaurant. What remained of the chicken no doubt became the base of the forcemeat for the *quenelles* that were made freshly each morning.

STEAMED CHICKEN MÈRE FILLIOUX

The very best quality of chicken was used for steaming, as we use the best steel for gadgets, which is a very smart thing to do. The chicken has very thin slices of truffles slipped with a sharp knife between the skin and the flesh, and before trussing it the cavity is filled with truffles. Place the bird in the steamer over half white wine and half veal broth with salt and pepper and the juice of a lemon. The latter will give a flavour, but above all will keep the chicken white. The chicken was gigantic but so young that less than an hour had sufficed to cook it. This she told me when she came to carve it. She looked at it critically, then proudly. She was an artist.

Aunt Pauline eventually got us to Perpignan where we settled down to work. At the quiet hotel we had selected there was a banquet hall, closed for the duration of the war. I made arrangements to use it as a depot from which to distribute, the greater part to serve as a warehouse for the material already awaiting us at the station, and a corner to be screened off to serve us as an office where we could receive doctors and nurses who would come with lists of their individual needs. The hotel was delightful. There were wartime restrictions, and a few privations, but each guest was hoveringly cared for by one or more members of a family of four. The cooking was excellent, southern – not Provençal but Catalan. The Roussillon had been French for little more than 150 years. One of the local dishes was a dessert frequently served called

MILLASON

Pour slowly 2 cups boiling milk over 1½ cups white cornflour and 1 cup sugar. Stir carefully to prevent lumps from forming. The mixture must be quite smooth. Boil stirring constantly about 20 minutes until quite stiff. Turn into a bowl, add 2 well-beaten eggs, 4 tablespoons melted butter, and 1 tablespoon orange-flower water. Pour on to buttered platter and when cool enough to handle form into cakes and fry in oil in frying pan until golden on each side. Sprinkle with powdered sugar and serve at once.

They made the *millason* very large at Perpignan. They would be daintier if smaller. They are, surprisingly, not unlike our Southern fried corn bread.

The little lobsters in Perpignan were common, cheap, and tender. They were cooked with a thick rich sauce and one day the very young waiter about to be mobilized was so eager to please that in rushing to serve us he all but spilled the sauce over my new uniform, of which I was inordinately proud.

PERPIGNAN LOBSTER

Cook 4 small lobsters not weighing more than 1 lb. each in boiling water, salted, for 18 or 20 minutes. During this time melt in a saucepan 4 tablespoons butter and heat in it 1 large carrot cut in thin rings and 2 medium-sized onions with a clove stuck on one of them and the white of 1 leek. When they are coated in butter sprinkle 1 tablespoon flour over them, mix well. Add little by little 1 cup hot dry white wine and 1 cup hot *bouillon*,* 1 large bouquet of parsley, fennel and basil, salt, pepper, a pinch of cayenne, a pinch of saffron, 4 cloves of crushed garlic, and 4 tablespoons tomato *purée*. Cover and cook slowly for 1 hour. Cut the lobsters longitudinally, take out the meat and place the 8 pieces in a hot casserole, take out the meat from the claws and place in the interstices of the lobster meat in the casserole. Take out of the sauce parsley, fennel, and basil if you wish. They did not in Perpignan. Pour the sauce over the lobster meat into the casserole. Serve piping hot.

There had been difficulty in getting gasoline on the coupons the army gave us. The major who was in charge of this distribution had been very helpful. Gertrude Stein

---

* *Bouillon* is a 'boiling', a stock made of veal, chicken, or beef bones simmered in water with the special vegetables and herbs appropriate to the dish.

did not like going to offices – she said they, army or civilian, were obnoxious. To replace her, I had introduced myself with her official papers and had allowed the major to call me Miss Stein. What difference could it make to him. We were just two Americans working for French wounded. By the time the difficulties had been overcome we had become quite friendly. At the last visit he said, Miss Stein, my wife and I want to know if you both want to dine with us some evening. It was time to acknowledge who I was. He drew back in his chair and with a violence that alarmed me said, Madame, there is something sinister in this affair. My explanation did not completely reassure him, but Gertrude Stein waiting in Aunt Pauline in the street below would. I asked him if he wouldn't go down with me to meet her. He did. Her cheerful innocence was convincing, and his invitation was repeated and accepted. They were delightful. Madame de B. was training a local cook to cook as she believed cooking should be done.

During wars, no game is allowed to be shot in France except boar that come down into the fields and do great damage. To prevent this a permit is given to landowners to shoot them on their property. A farmer had shot one and brought the saddle to Madame de B. So we had

ROASTED SADDLE OF YOUNG BOAR

Even young boar is put in a marinade. One carrot and 1 onion cut in rings, 2 shallots cut in half, salt, pepper, a very large bunch of rosemary with just enough good dry red wine to cover the saddle is all that is needed for a light marinade. Four hours in the marinade turning the meat twice will suffice. An hour before it is time to put in the oven, take the saddle from the marinade and dry thoroughly. Strain the marinade into a saucepan, discard the vegetables but retain the branch of rosemary. For roasting allow 18 minutes a lb. in a 450° oven for the first 20 minutes, reduce to 350°. Roasting meat in an earthenware dish that can be brought to the table is a time-saver. Put a piece of butter in the dish that when melted will amply cover the dish. When the butter bubbles, place the saddle in the dish with 3 tablespoons melted butter on the meat. After 20 minutes baste with the branch of rosemary. If there is not enough melted butter and juice in the dish add 4 or 5 tablespoons hot marinade. Baste every 12 minutes, adding hot marinade as needed. While the roast is in the oven peel, boil, and skin enough chestnuts to garnish the roast with a double wreath of them. Skim the juice before adding the chestnuts. Allow the chestnuts to cook in the skimmed juice for 15 minutes. Then serve in a sauce boat at the same time this:

GAME SAUCE

Melt 1½ tablespoons butter in a saucepan until it is golden brown, add 1 tablespoon flour, stir until light brown. Add slowly over low heat 1 cup of the hot marinade, the juice of 1 lemon, 1 tablespoon grated lemon peel, 1 tablespoon grated orange peel, a good pinch of cayenne, ¾ cup currant jelly.

Venison may be cooked in the same way and pork is particularly good in this manner, except that the marinade should be of good dry white wine and the meat remain in it for 24 hours, turning four or five times. The game sauce is required for boar or venison, but should not be served with pork.

In one of the dark narrow back streets of Perpignan there was a small, remarkably good restaurant whose reputation was well known in Paris. After an excellent lunch we decided to ask Madame de B. and the Major to dine with us. Consulting with the *chef,* this was the menu decided upon:

Creamed chicken soup à la Reine Margot
Spring duckling with
Asparagus with Virgin Sauce
Coupe Dino

The *chef* generously gave me the recipe for Virgin Sauce which accompanied the steamed green asparagus.

VIRGIN SAUCE

For 1 person, place 5 tablespoons butter in a hot bowl, add ¼ teaspoon salt, beat with a whisk until the butter foams, put it over hot but not boiling water for an instant. The butter must not melt. When the butter foams, add drop by drop, never ceasing to whisk 1 teaspoon lemon juice and 1 tablespoon tepid water. When they are well amalgamated with the foaming butter, add

1 tablespoon whipped cream and serve at once. This sauce is delicious with cold fish. It is something apart.

We had visited all the hospitals in the region and had reported on their future needs. Having made our last distributions we closed the depot at Perpignan and returned to Paris for another assignment. By this time, 1917, the United States had broken relations with Germany and had declared war. At last we were no longer neutral. On the road to Nevers, as Gertrude Stein was changing spark plugs – and when was one not in those days – we were told that a detachment of Marines was expected there that afternoon. Aunt Pauline was pushed to her utmost speed that we might be there for the entry. Thrilled by the first sight of the doughboys, we were unprepared for their youth, vigour, and gaiety compared to the fatigue and exhaustion of the French soldiers. We were asked by some of their officers to meet the soldiers that evening and tell them about France. They had dozens of questions to ask, but what they wanted most to know was how many miles they were from the front and why the French trucks made such a noise. Though they were disappointed in our answers we had a wonderful and exciting evening together. It was their first contact with France and ours with our army.

In Paris the A.F.F.W. proposed we should open a depot at Nîmes where in advance of our arrival they would send several car-loads of material. News of our household was not so encouraging. During our absence our competent faithful Jeanne had gotten herself married. An excellent cook who worked by the hour consented to spend with us the few days we were to be in Paris. Severe rationing of meat, butter, eggs, gas, and electricity had gone into effect. A small reserve of coal and assorted candles gave meagre heat and light. Ernestine accomplished much with little which permitted us to ask for lunch some of the Field Service men and volunteer nurses on leave in Paris. For them she made

KNEPPES

Remove skin and nerves from 1 lb. calves' liver, chop very fine, pound into paste, add 3 crushed shallots and 1 clove of garlic previously heated in butter, salt, pepper, 3 tablespoons flour, a pinch of mace, and mix thoroughly. Add one at a time the yolks of 2 eggs. When well amalgamated add gently the whites of 2 eggs well beaten but not dry. Drop by tablespoons into boiling salted water, and boil for ½ hour. They will rise to the surface. Drain thoroughly. Place on serving dish and pour over them ½ cup browned butter and 2 tablespoons dry breadcrumbs.

Ernestine said she learned this dish from a Belgian cook but we suspected he was of Alsatian origin. She also made for us

SWEETBREADS À LA NAPOLITAINE

Soak a pair of sweetbreads in cold water for an hour. Rinse and boil for 10 minutes in salted water. Rinse, remove all skin, cut into thin slices, and brown lightly in 4 tablespoons butter in a saucepan. Add 1 cup sherry,

1 cup *bouillon*, 1 tablespoon tomato *purée*, salt, pepper, ½ cup diced ham. Place slices of sweetbread in this sauce. Cover and cook over low flame for 20 minutes. Prepare 4 thin slices Bologna sausage chopped fine, 1 large chopped onion, brown together in 2 tablespoons butter in an iron pot, add ½ lb. well-washed rice, turn with wooden spoon until rice is covered with butter. Add 1 cup boiling *bouillon*. Continue to stir until *bouillon* is absorbed, then add ¼ lb. finely chopped mushrooms and 1 tablespoon *purée* of tomatoes, add 1 cup boiling *bouillon*, salt, pepper, a pinch of saffron. Continue to turn with fork slowly adding 2 more cups hot *bouillon*, 1 quart in all. When the rice has absorbed all the *bouillon*, it should be sufficiently cooked. Add ½ cup grated parmesan cheese and serve with sweetbreads.

The luxury hotel at Nîmes was in a sad way. The proprietor had been killed at the war, the *chef* was mobilized, the food was poor and monotonous. Aunt Pauline had been militarized and so could be requisitioned for any use connected with the wounded. Gertrude Stein evacuated the wounded who came into Nîmes on the ambulance trains. Material from our unit organized and supplied a small first-aid operating room. The Red Cross nuns in the best French manner served in large bowls to the wounded, piping

HOT CHOCOLATE

3 oz. melted chocolate to 1 quart hot milk. Bring to a boil and simmer for ½ hour. Then beat for 5 minutes. The nuns made huge quantities in copper cauldrons, so

that the whisk they used was huge and heavy. We all
took turns in beating.

Monsieur le Préfet and his wife, *Madame la Préfet*, whom
we got to know and to like a lot, sent us word that a regi-
ment of American soldiers was expected, that a camp
was being prepared for them, and that he would like us
to be at the station with him when they arrived. Nîmes
was agog with excitement and welcomed them as best it
could – green wreaths, bunting, and flags. Thanksgiving
Day was some ten days after the soldiers arrived. Even
the most modest homes were inviting our soldiers to
lunch or to dinner to celebrate the day. That evening we
had for dinner a large tableful of soldiers from camp.
The manageress of the hotel, a large buxom blonde, had
a group of American officers at her table. They were
perhaps too noticeably gay.

At dinner one night – the inevitable whiting with its
tail in its mouth was our monotonous fare – what
appeared undoubtedly to be a German passed our table.
This is really going too far, I said to Gertrude Stein. How
dare an escaped prisoner show himself so publicly, so
brazenly. Not your affair, let the authorities deal with
him, she answered. After dinner the too-gay manageress
said to me, There is a gentleman who has been asking to
speak to you. I will send for him. It was the German. In
perfect English he said he wished to speak to us alone a
moment, and he pointed to some chairs. Gertrude Stein,
always cheerful, agreeable, and curious, sat down but
not I. Who are you and what do you want of us, I asked.
I do want some information from you, but first let me

introduce myself. I am Samuel Barlow and we have several friends in common, but I am here as an officer in the secret service, in civvies naturally, to find out what is going on between younder gay blonde and the American officers. The *Préfet* reported the case to us. He says he has reason to believe she is a German. Well, said I relieved, rather she than you. I mistook you for a German. My only civilian clothes, he said, were from Germany where I was a prisoner. This ended my concern with escaping German prisoners.

At Christmas the English wife of a prominent Nîmois organized, with the aid of the English companions and governesses who had posts in Nîmes, a dinner and dance for the British convalescent officers and men stationed there, and requisitioning for their army at Arles. After dinner we took turns dancing with the men. It was as gay as we could make it but the British Army was not cheerful. A few days later I had a visit from the prettiest of the young governesses. She said there had been an unfortunate incident after the party was over. She was preparing to turn out the light in her bedroom when there was a tap on the door which evidently connected with another room, and a voice asked, I say, Miss L., should I light my fire. Too surprised to answer, she was silent for a moment. The question was repeated, I say, Miss L., should I light my fire. Not for me, thank you, she answered. Of course the voice was unrecognizable, she ended, so I will never know which one of them it was.

Suddenly one day there was the Armistice and a telegram from the *Comité* – If you speak German, close the depot immediately, return to proceed Alsace civilian relief. If we had missed the spontaneous outburst of joy in Paris on Armistice Day we were going into liberated Alsace. One starlit morning we started in Auntie to make the six hundred odd kilometres to Paris before night. Gertrude Stein ate her share of bread and butter and roast chicken while driving. Paris was still celebrating, and here the streets were commencing to be filled with the French Army, on the move into occupied Germany, and a certain number of Allied officers and men.

Having secured a German-French dictionary and fur-lined aviator's jackets and gloves, cumbersome but warm, we got off on the road again. The French Army was moving in the same direction Auntie was taking us. Near Tulle the mules dragging the regimental kitchen became unruly, swerved to the left, and bumped into Auntie. A mudguard, the tool box, and its contents scattered on the road and into the ditch. There was, of course, no way of recovering them. Starting off again, Gertrude Stein found the triangle so damaged as to make driving on the icy road not only difficult but possibly dangerous. We got to Nancy exhausted, too late for dinner, but Dorothy Wilde sweetly found two hard-boiled ducks' eggs, a novel but very satisfying repast. While Auntie was being repaired next day at the garage of the *Comité*, we had our first meal without restrictions. For a first course we were served

QUÈCHE DE NANCY

Prepare the evening before baking a pie crust made with 1 cup and 2 tablespoons flour, 5 tablespoons butter, a

37

pinch of salt, 4 tablespoons water. The butter should be worked into the flour lightly but the mixture need be no finer than rice. Roll on a slightly floured board into a ball, cover with waxed paper, and put aside for at least 12 hours. Then roll lightly and fit into deep pie plate 9 inches in diameter. Place on the crust ½ cup cubed ham. Remove the skin from lean salt pork, cube 5 oz., and place on crust having previously cooked the cubes in boiling water for 10 minutes, drained them, and wiped them dry. Beat 3 eggs, pepper, and salt, with ½ cup cream. Pour over ham and salt pork in pie crust. Dot with 12 small pieces of butter. Bake in preheated 450° oven for 15 minutes, reduce heat to 300° and bake for 20 minutes more. Remove from oven but not from pie plate for 10 minutes.

After which Aunt Pauline took us through no-man's-land to Strasbourg, still celebrating the Liberation. That night there was a torchlight procession of soldiers and civilians, the young girls in their attractive costumes (the black ribbon head-dress they had worn since 1870 changed to all the colours of the rainbow), with military bands. It was more like a dream than a reality. We were now in the land of plenty.

The next morning the director of civilian relief sent us to Mulhouse, the centre of the devastated area. Our material was already waiting there, and we got to work at once. For several days we unpacked the material, saw mayors, clergymen, and priests from the ruined villages to which the refugees were returning on foot, by trucks, by any means they could find. It was very sad.

Their determination and courage, however, were very heartening. We settled down to a winter of outdoor distributing to each village in turn. At Mulhouse we were not uncomfortable, first in the large hotel, then when that was requisitioned for officers in a purely Alsatian inn. There was an abundance of food, real coffee, large hams, real milk. Queues formed to look at them and buy them. The *pâtisseries* were filled with specialities of Alsace and the classic cakes of France. The French soldiers ate unlimited quantities and even sent them to their families and friends in France. At our inn they made a most satisfactory

SOUP OF SHALLOTS AND CHEESE

For each person lightly brown in butter on each side 1 slice of bread. Put in soup tureen, sprinkle with 1 tablespoon grated cheese, and keep hot. Cook over low flame 4 sliced shallots in 1 tablespoon butter, add 1 teaspoon flour. Stir with wooden spoon, add 1½ cups hot *bouillon*, cook covered over lowest flame, add salt and pepper, for ½ hour. Strain, add 2 tablespoons cream. Pour over bread and cheese in tureen and serve hot.

The quality of the material was excellent but there was no variety in the vegetables. They were all of the cabbage family, sauerkraut, cabbage, brussels sprouts, and cauliflower. There were potatoes, to be sure, and apple sauce, which was considered a vegetable.

At Cernay we were helped in our distribution by little Abbé Hick, who had returned after the Armistice to find his church bombed, and the presbytery with the exception of one room in ruins. He asked us however to lunch with him the next time we were distributing in his neighbourhood. He met us at the door of his room and said, Welcome, come into the salon and warm yourselves. Excuse me while I go into the bedroom and wash my hands. He went to the far end of the room past a set dining-room table. Presently he returned and said, Now we will go into the dining-room and have lunch. All this without the least suspicion of the ludicrous. A refugee had cooked the simple but succulent lunch. The Abbé's mother had sent him some good white wine from Riquewehr where she lived.

On Sundays we frequently lunched with the hospitable Mulhouséens who were gradually returning to the lives they had led before the war. Everything was in the French manner, with great elegance and luxury. They had really kept the manner of living of pre-1870. They had refused everything German. It was the memory of the way our French friends in San Francisco had lived come to life again.

At Monsieur B.'s there was for dessert, to my delight, a

TARTE CHAMBORD

Beat until foamy and thick with a rotary beater 1 cup and 1 tablespoon sugar and 8 eggs, gently stir in 2 cups and 3 tablespoons thrice-sifted flour. Add 1 cup and 1 tablespoon melted unsalted butter. Bake in a deep buttered and floured cake pan in 350° preheated oven for 30 minutes. Take from oven, let stand for 10 minutes, take out of pan, place on grill. When cold, cut horizontally four times, making five layers.

CREAM FOR CAKE

Turn with a wooden spoon in an enamelled saucepan the yolks of 10 eggs and very slowly add 1½ cups icing sugar. Turn until thick and pale yellow. Put over lowest flame with 4 tablespoons butter for 2 minutes and as soon as butter is melted, stirring constantly, remove from flame and when the mixture is cold add drop by drop 3 tablespoons cold water. Return to flame stirring until the mixture is even. Remove from flame and when the cream is cold add drop by drop ¼ cup kirsch or curaçao. Cover the layers and re-form the cake. Cover the top and sides with the cream and put in the refrigerator.

COFFEE FROSTING

In an enamelled saucepan put ¾ cup very strong black coffee. Add enough icing sugar to make a very heavy cream. Warm over low heat. Pour on cake and with a spatula cover top and sides of cake. Sprinkle thickly with finely ground pistachio nuts.

We worked very hard all that cold winter distributing in the open air. Then one day there were fruit blossoms and storks. By this time the refugee relief was organized by the Government. We closed the depot, said good-bye to the officials and the people we had met, and started off for Metz to see the battlefields of 1870 and to see

Verdun. It was still a shambles. We wandered about locating the spots where the defence of the *poilus* had made history. It was the middle of the afternoon when Gertrude Stein finally asked, Where did you say we were going to lunch. I've gotten hungry. We got into Aunt Pauline and made our way slowly over the fields to something that had been a road. There we came upon a military car filled with officers. They said if we followed them we could find something to eat – in fact, they were eating there. They stopped at a corrugated iron hut and sure enough the man who presumably lived there made us an omelette with fried potatoes and a cup of real coffee, so rare in those days that at once I realized that the officers must have brought their own provisions with them and that we were sharing them. And then I remembered the two boxes of cakes the Abbé's mother had sent to us the day before. So we got them out of Auntie. The little Alsatian cakes were of her own baking and delicious. We took a few of each kind and gave the rest to the officers whose unwitting guests we had been. These are their recipes.

SCHANKELE OR SCHENKELE

Cream ½ cup butter, add slowly ½ cup sugar, add slowly 4 eggs, one at a time. Add about 5 cups flour, depending upon size of eggs, with 1 teaspoon baking powder and 1 cup skinned and very finely ground almonds. The dough should be just firm enough to hold its shape when rolled in the hands into finger-length sausages. Fry in deep lard only enough of the cakes to cover the surface. Turn once to brown on both sides. Take from fat and place on absorbent paper. Sprinkle while still hot with plenty of icing sugar. They are a nice accompaniment to a glass of white wine or a cup of coffee. They keep well in a well-covered box.

LAEKERLIS

The Alsatians claim that Laekerlis are their creation, but the Swiss answer that they have two different kinds, one from Berne and one from Basle. This is Madame Hick's from Riquewehr. Warm 2 lb. honey and skim, add 3 cups and 3 tablespoons sugar, 1 teaspoon cinnamon, ½ teaspoon cloves, ¼ teaspoon powdered cardamom, ½ teaspoon all-spice, 1 teaspoon mace, ¼ teaspoon powdered anise, 1 cup finely chopped orange peel, ¼ cup finely chopped lemon peel, ½ cup finely chopped citron, and 2 cups finely chopped almonds. Mix thoroughly and gradually work in 7 cups sifted flour. Roll on a lightly floured board to ⅓-inch thickness. Cut in rectangles, place on lightly buttered baking sheet. If you have not a number of baking sheets, roll out the dough and leave on the floured board. Put aside for 24 hours in a temperate room and then bake in 350° oven. When baked, remove from baking sheet and place on grill. While still warm, paint with brush with this mixture:

Dissolve over very low flame 2 cups sugar and 3 tablespoons hot water. If this crystallizes during the time the Lackerlis are baking, add a little hot water. These are of long conservation, as the French say.

We were lunching the next day with our friends from Nîmes, Madame T. and the *Préfet*, who were now installed at the *Préfecture* of Châlons-sur-Marne. We spent the night at the Hôtel Mère Dieu – a sacrilege in English. Châlons-sur-Marne is near Reims and the wine cellar of the *Préfecture* is supplied by the Government with the best wines of the region. Lunch was served with ceremony and elegance worthy of the menu, the cooking and the wines. Of the menu I only remember the

SADDLE OF MUTTON MAINTENON

Put a saddle of mutton with salt, pepper, and 3 tablespoons butter in a Dutch oven covered in a 350° oven. Turn every 10 minutes. Allow 10 minutes per lb. for the cooking of the saddle. When it is three-quarters cooked, remove from oven, place the meat on a carving board, and with a very sharp knife slice very thinly both sides of the saddle. Be careful to lose none of the juice. Having cooked 1 chopped onion in butter, put it into ¾ cup stiff Béchamel sauce with ½ cup chopped mushrooms cooked for 5 minutes in butter. Mix these ingredients thoroughly, spread on each slice of mutton, replace the slices on the saddle. Cover the saddle with three chopped onions, melted butter, breadcrumbs, more melted butter. Skim the juice in the Dutch oven, pour into preheated earthenware dish, place the saddle in the juice and the dish into a quick oven to brown the meat.

With this serve hearts of artichokes and small boiled potatoes *maître d'hôtel*.

As we were leaving the *Préfecture*, Gertrude Stein confided to me that she was going to show me a tank that the *Préfet* had told her was still in a field on the road to Reims. It would not be much out of our way and it was certainly worth seeing.

Auntie took fields so well. As we went along the national highway, Auntie and her driver were happily swaying and serpentining along. The wine at lunch was undoubtedly to blame for their lack of responsibility. They nevertheless negotiated the field. We saw the tank and got on our way to spend the night with Mildred Aldrich at the Hillcrest. It was from there she had seen the first Battle of the Marne and the German retreat. In her garden that evening I wrote the last report to the *Comité*.

The next morning we were back in Paris, more beautiful, vital, and inextinguishable than ever. We commenced madly running about, to see our friends and theirs. It was gay, a little feverish, but pleasurably exciting. Auntie Pauline took us to lunch and dinner parties. Our home was filled with people coming and going. We spoke of each other as the chauffeur and the cook. We had no servant. We had largely overdrawn at our banks to supply the needs of soldiers and their families and now the day of reckoning had come. We would live like gypsies, go everywhere in left-over finery, with a *pot-au-feu* for the many friends we should be seeing. Paris was filled with Allies, the Armies, the Peace Commission, and anyone who could get a passport. We lunched and dined with a great many of them, at their messes, headquarters, homes, and restaurants.

One evening Aunt Pauline had taken us out to the Bois de Boulogne to dine with friends in the garden of one of its restaurants. While dinner was being served the *maître d'hôtel* asked me to please follow him, someone wished to speak to me. It was a policeman to announce that trucks were not allowed in the Bois. They had been tolerated during the war, but an Armistice had been signed. So would Madame see that her truck did not appear there again. When I got back to the table an excellent dish was being served.

HARICOT

(yes, that is its seventeenth-century name)

Take an oxtail, separate the joints, put them in a pot with some marrow, salt, 1 clove, a twig of sage, 1 laurel leaf, and a little water. When the meat is half cooked add 1 lb. sliced turnips, 1 lb. peeled and skinned chestnuts, and 10 slices of any highly spiced sausage. Cook until the meat is tender and the juice reduced. Then add 8 slices of toast on which 3 tablespoons vinegar have been sprinkled. There are some who like a few prunes or raisins added. Our haricot's sauce had raisins in it. They had previously been swollen by soaking in hot water. They are an agreeable addition and cut the acid of the vinegar.

In the spring of 1919 we went to Normandy to stay with friends. A calf that they wished to sell at the local fair was put into Auntie, and she brought the first potato harvest to market, so that a thorough cleaning of Auntie was required on our return. On the way to Paris we stopped at Duclair. The hotel was on the Seine, its cooking was famous. It was there we had

SOLE DE LA MAISON

Poach gently in milk the fillets of sole with salt and pepper. Cover and simmer gently for about 15 minutes, depending upon the thickness of the fillets. Drain thoroughly. Place on a preheated carving dish and keep hot. Poach only long enough to heat 4 oysters and 4 large shrimps for each fillet. Place them alternately on the fillet. Cover with heavy cream sauce made with heavy cream and flavoured with 2 tablespoons best dry sherry.

At Duclair everything was cooked in cream: chicken, cabbages, indeed all vegetables and most meats. We stayed there several days before this bored us. At nearby Rouen butter replaced the cream. The butter was of such an excellent quality that it seemed advisable to make arrangements to have a weekly delivery to us in Paris. At a recommended creamery this was discouraged. Parcel post was not yet reliable. So I bought 12 lb. to take back to friends and for our use. To my delight each pound was packed in a porous black earthenware jar of exactly the same form as the Gallo-Romain ones that we had been seeing in the museums. I kept two of them until last year when I gave them to a friend who would not believe they were not originals and that I was not parting with treasures.

When we returned to Paris our friends convinced us that the time had come to transform Auntie into something more suitable for the use we were making of her. The state of her engine did not warrant the purchase of a new body. We had her high canvas cover lowered so satisfactorily that we had her painted, but, neglecting to choose a colour, she returned to us painted a funereal black. This and her new form suggested a hearse – for an *enterrement de troisième classe*. She would continue to be *risible* to the end.

Gradually we realized that poor Auntie was weakening. It was no longer advisable to take her too far on the road. We would go to Mildred Aldrich's and in summer have a picnic lunch in her garden, and indoors in her cosy little home in winter when Amélie, her devoted friend, neighbour, and servant, would make us the very best we ever ate

CRÈME RENVERSÈE

Put 4 lumps of sugar in a metal pudding mould over a very low heat. When melted add 1½ teaspoons cold water. Turn the mould in all directions to cover it completely with the caramel. Heat 2 cups evaporated milk with ½ cup sugar. Put aside to cool. Stir 4 eggs until thoroughly mixed, add 2 teaspoons orange-flower water. Strain into the cold cream. Pour into prepared mould, set mould into pan of hot water reaching to half the height of the mould. Place in preheated 350° oven for 40 minutes. The water should not boil. When a knife gently stuck into the *crème* comes out dry, remove from oven and remove mould from water. Do not attempt to turn out of mould until cold. This is very nice served with chocolate sauce.

I was aghast to find Amélie using tinned milk in a country of excellent fresh milk. She explained that it was the milk Madame's friends had sent her in such quantities after the war. She assured me that even fresh milk did not adequately replace it. It was the only time in my experience that a French woman recommended American tinned products to replace French fresh ones.

Auntie held out for another year and then one day as we were passing the entrance to the Palais du Luxembourg she stopped short. Nothing Gertrude Stein did was of any avail, she would not budge. We were quickly surrounded by an amused crowd and by half a dozen not at all amused policemen. One of them asked if we didn't know that it was an infraction of the law to obstruct the entrance to a public building, particularly the Senate, where the Prime Minister was expected any minute to drive through. Indeed soldiers on motor bicycles had already arrived and a large car was was being held back. We jumped out of Auntie, the police shoved her out of the way, and the big car passed through with Monsieur Poincaré's beautiful head out of the window to see the cause of the commotion. We basely deserted Auntie and went home on foot. Gertrude Stein telephoned to the garage to haul her in and repair her at once. The answer next day was that she was beyond repair. Nothing daunted, Gertrude Stein went to the garage with our good friend, Georges Maratier. She wanted his help and his advice to realize it. He said the two of them would drive to the country garage of his parents where there was plenty of room. There Auntie would be an honoured war souvenir. Her odyssey was the subject of the following winter's conversation. She is still there, but I have never had the courage to go to see her.

At no matter what sacrifice it was unthinkable that we should be without a car. Fords were still scare in France, but Gertrude Stein inveigled a promise that she would have a two-seater open one within two weeks. As we were driving her to a beautiful new box fortunately secured in our neighbourhood for her I remarked that she was nude. There was nothing on her dashboard, neither clock nor ashbox, nor cigarette lighter. Godiva, was Gertrude Stein's answer. The new car was baptized without benefit of clergy or even a glass of wine. The reason for her name soon disappeared with all the gifts she received, but Godiva remained her name.

Now we would go on excursions out of town again. On the road to Chartres we made acquaintance with an excellent little restaurant which unfortunately disappeared during the Occupation of the second war. There we ate

CHICKEN SAUTÉ À LA FORESTIÈRE

Put the chicken with 3 tablespoons butter in a Dutch oven over medium heat, keep turning it about. When lightly browned on all sides reduce heat and cover, in ¼ hour add ½ lb. morels previously cooked in tepid water, brushed, and well rinsed, ⅓ lb. pig's fat cooked previously for 5 minutes in boiling water and well drained, salt, pepper. Cover and simmer over low flame for ¾ hour, depending upon size of chicken. When done remove from flame, place chicken on preheated serving dish, remove morels from sauce with perforated spoon, and place around chicken. Skim juice and return pot to stove, add 1 cup good dry white wine and ½ cup stock. Boil uncovered for 5 minutes. Strain and pour over chicken. New potatoes browned in butter are almost obligatory for this dish.

Godiva took us to Orleans where on the banks of the Loire we ate freshly caught

SALMON WITH SAUCE HOLLANDAISE AU BEURRE NOISETTE

The salmon was cold, decorated with tomatoes, hard-boiled eggs (yolks and whites) pounded in a mortar separately, and thinly sliced cucumbers.

THE SAUCE

Sauce Hollandaise is easily and quickly prepared if you pay careful attention to this foolproof recipe. Put 4 yolks of eggs and a little pepper and salt in a small saucepan over the lowest possible flame. Stir continuously with a wooden spoon, adding drop by drop ½ lb. browned butter. Put ¾ cup shelled hazel nuts in the oven. When they are warm remove from oven and roll in a cloth until all the skins are removed. Pound them in a mortar to a powder, adding from time to time a few drops of water to prevent the nuts from exuding oil. Strain through hair sieve. Replace in mortar and add 1 cup water. Mix with pestle or wooden spoon. When perfectly amalgamated commence to add in very small quantities at a time to the egg yolks in the saucepan, stirring continuously. If the contents of pan become too hot remove a moment from flame and add a small quantity of butter to cool the mixture before replacing over flame. When all the butter has been incorporated remove from flame and slowly stir into the sauce 1 tablespoon vinegar. Serve in sauce boat.

This is a rare sauce. Once the hazel nuts are prepared it takes little time to prepare. Do not take the time to think that almonds can successfully replace the hazel nuts which give the sauce its elusive and distinctive flavour.

Even though Godiva was what a friend ironically called a gentleman's car, she took us into the woods and fields as Auntie had. We gathered the early wild flowers, violets at Versailles, daffodils at Fontainebleau, hyacinths (the bluebells of Scotland) in the forest of Saint Germain. For these excursions there were two picnic lunches I used to prepare.

FIRST PICNIC LUNCH

A chicken is simmered in white wine with salt and paprika. Ten minutes before the chicken is sufficiently cooked add ½ cup finely chopped mushrooms. When cooked remove chicken and drain. Strain mushrooms.

The juice may be kept in the refrigerator to be used as stock. Put the mushrooms in a bowl, add an equal quantity of butter and work into a paste. This is very good as a sandwich spread or may be thoroughly mixed with the yolks of 3 hard-boiled eggs and put into the hard-boiled eggs which have been cut in half.

For dessert fill cream-puff shells with crushed sweetened strawberries.

SECOND PICNIC LUNCH

One cup finely chopped roast rare beef, 1 teaspoon chopped parsley, 1 teaspoon crushed shallots, salt, pepper, 1 teaspoon tomato *purée*, 1 tablespoon sour cream, a pinch of dry mustard. Mix thoroughly. Lightly toast on one side only eight slices of bread. Butter generously the untoasted sides. Spread on the buttered side of four slices of the bread the meat mixture. Cover, with buttered side over meat, with the other four slices of bread.

To eat with these sandwiches, prepare lettuce leaves on which boiled diced sweetbreads are placed, 1½ cups for four large lettuce leaves. On the sweetbreads place 4 chopped truffles that have been cooked in sherry. Roll the lettuce leaves round the sweetbreads and truffles, neatly trim with scissors and tie with white kitchen string in three places.

For dessert peel apples, core, cut in half and caramelize in ¾ cup sugar and ¼ cup water that has boiled to the caramel stage, for about 10 minutes. Completely coat the apples with the caramel. When dry wrap in square of puff paste, moistening the edges so that they will adhere. Fry in deep fat until golden brown on all sides. Remove from fat to absorbent paper. While still hot cover generously with sifted icing sugar. Excellent hot or cold.

Godiva had been taking us successfully to places in the neighbourhood of Paris. It was time to give her a wider field. In early spring she would take us to the Côte d'Azur. We had been asked to stay with a friend at Vence. We would wander down the Rhône Valley and see to what she would lead us. We would start early and spend the night at Saulieu to which Auntie had taken us several years before. To look at the church when we got there we parked Godiva in the square about 100 feet from the hotel. When we returned Godiva flatly refused to start. What were we to do. A red-liveried groom appeared and asked if he could help. Perhaps if he pushed the car – which he did. Godiva's engine started. Before we knew what she was up to we were in the court of what turned out to be the rival hotel of the one we intended to go to. It was her first display of instinct to lead us to the real right place. It must be acknowledged that never later did she shine with equal lustre.

The Côte d'Or then had as its proprietor and *chef* a quite fabulous person. First of all he looked like a great Clouet portrait, a museum piece. He had great experience and knowledge of the history of French cooking from the time of Clouet to the present. From him I learned a great deal. At dinner that evening we realized that he was one of the great French *chefs*. Each dish had a simplicity and a perfection. Comparing the cooking of a dish to the painting of a picture, it has always seemed to me that however much the cook or painter did to cover any weakness would not in the least avail. Such devices would only emphasize the weakness. There was no weak spot in the food prepared by the *chef* at the Hôtel de la Côte d'Or.

For dinner we had

MORVAN HAM WITH CREAM SAUCE

Four thick slices of ham from which the skin but not the rind has been removed are placed in a saucepan and browned lightly in butter with 1 onion, 1 carrot, 1 leek, and the greens of 6 radishes. Add ½ cup Madeira or good dry sherry and 1½ cups *bouillon*, salt, pepper, and 1 crushed shallot. Cover and cook over very low flame for 2 hours. Be careful that it does not burn. If the pan is hermetically covered this will not happen. If not, it may be necessary to add more wine and *bouillon* in the above proportions. At the end of 2 hours remove from flame. Strain juice, reject vegetables, put ham aside. Skim juice and place ¾ cup over medium heat uncovered. Reduce to ½ cup and place ham in saucepan. Glaze on both sides. Add rest of strained juice and 1 cup heavy cream. Bring to a boil and simmer for 2 minutes, tipping the saucepan in all directions.

Saulieu is in the Morvan, an old division of France and part of Burgundy and has always been famous for its ham, which is not unlike York ham.

We stayed on next day for lunch and again chose a simple dish –

THREE-MINUTE VEAL STEAK

Ask the butcher to cut very thin slices in a fillet of veal, remove bones, skin, and fat. It is well to count upon two slices per person, eight slices for four people. Brown on both sides in ¼ cup butter in Dutch oven over high flame, salt and pepper. When they are brown, cover and put in preheated over at 400° for 5 minutes. Add 1 cup hot dry white wine. Take meat from oven and place on preheated serving dish. Skim juice, place over high flame, and mix well with glaze at the bottom and sides. Reduce heat to very low, add in small pieces 6 tablespoons butter, shaking pot in all directions. Add a squeeze of lemon juice and pour over meat and sprinkle 4 tablespoons chopped parsley over meat and sauce. This is delicious if the preparation is not allowed to drag.

At Mâcon that evening for dinner we had

PURÉE OF ARTICHOKE SOUP

Wash thoroughly 6 large artichokes, cut them in half vertically, and remove chokes with a sharp knife. Put 3 tablespoons butter in a saucepan. When melted add artichokes. Stir them with wooden spoon until well covered with butter. Add 3 cups hot water and 3 cups hot chicken broth. Cover and boil steadily for 1 hour. Then add 2 cups thickly sliced potatoes. Cook for ½ hour more. Remove from fire and with a silver spoon scrape from all the leaves all the edible bits of artichoke. Crush this with the hearts and potatoes through a hair sieve with a potato masher. Strain juice in pan and add to strained artichokes and potatoes. Wash pan and place strained material in it. Heat over medium flame. If too thick add more chicken broth. Add salt and pepper. Before serving reduce heat and add 1 cup butter in small pieces. Tip saucepan in all directions and serve in pre-heated tureen in which you have placed very small unbuttered *croûtons*. This soup is well worth the effort and time it takes to make it.

The *chef* at Mâcon was proud of his desserts. They were delicious, varied, and abundant. He would come to your table as one after another was presented and his feelings would be hurt if you did not at least taste each one of them. There were always chocolate, coffee (or mocha), caramel, and pistachio creams and ice creams, berries in season with heavy but unwhipped cream in which a spoon stood upright, *tartes* of all kinds and one cake – a *Gâteau de la Maison*. For years this cake was a puzzlement to me. It wasn't until Lord Berners brought us one to Bilignin one summer when he was going to stay with us that I had enough courage to attempt an approach to the famous cake. How he had inveigled that cake out of the Mâcon hotel was not explained, but one suspected. This is as near as my experiments got me to

THE MÂCON CAKE

Brush four shallow-layer cake tins lightly with melted butter. At once sprinkle with sifted flour. Rap on back of tins to remove excess flour. Mix 1¼ cups powdered almonds and 1¼ cups sugar. Put aside. Put the whites of 8 eggs in a bowl and commence to beat them, gradually increasing the speed. Do not stop beating for an instant. When done they should form a stiff peak when whisk is removed. With a wooden spatula lightly mix in the sugar and powdered almonds. Fill the four layer pans and put at once in a preheated 300° oven for about ½ hour.

BUTTER CREAM FOR THREE LAYERS

Boil ¾ cup water with 1 cup sugar for 10 minutes. Stir yolks of 8 eggs for 5 minutes and slowly add syrup. Pour into double boiler stirring continuously with wooden spoon until spoon is coated. Strain through fine sieve beating vigorously until cool. Then add 1 cup whipped cream. Put 3 cups butter in a heated bowl and beat until creamy. Then very slowly add the syrup, yolks of eggs, whipped-cream mixture. Put aside.

MOCHA CREAM

Take a third of above mixture and drop by drop add 4 tablespoons very strong black coffee. Spread 1½ cups of this evenly on one of the meringue layers. Put aside the remaining mocha cream. Cover with another layer.

KIRSCH CREAM

Take another third of butter cream and add drop by drop 2 tablespoons best kirsch. Spread a third of this on layer of meringue covering mocha cream. Put aside the rest of kirsch cream. Cover kirsch cream with a third meringue layer.

PISTACHIO CREAM

Take the remaining third of butter cream and add ¾ cup thrice-ground pistachio nuts. Spread a third of this evenly on layer of meringue covering the kirsch cream, and cover with fourth and final layer of meringue. Reserve the rest of the pistachio for the crowning operation which is

TO DECORATE THE CAKE

Take remaining mocha cream and spread evenly over a third of top of cake and a third of the sides of cake. Spread evenly remaining kirsch over centre third of cake and centre third of sides of cake. Spread evenly remaining pistachio cream over remaining uncovered part of cake and sides. Now form a design in centre of cake about 2 inches in diameter of crystallized apricots and angelica. It is effective to make petals of the apricots with surrounding leaves of angelica. On the outside of the cake make very small flowers of the apricots with surrounding small angelica leaves, one little bouquet for each slice of cake. Keep in a cool place until time to serve. The meringue layers can be baked in advance. This is of course not a cake but a dessert. It has an elusive subtle flavour and is quite worth the time it takes to make it.

At Mâcon we heard of a very small but highly recommended restaurant at Grignan, a village of six hundred inhabitants in the Drôme, which is a department of France of fine cooking and romantic landscape. We wired to friends to meet us at Grignan for lunch. The name was familiar – was it not the name of Madame de Sévigné's adored daughter? In the guide book I found that the Château de Grignan was still intact, that one could visit it, and that Madame de Sévigné was buried in the church in the village. We would make a pilgrimage to the spot after lunch. When we arrived in the village and saw how small the restaurant was, we wondered if there would be room for the four of us. Madame Loubet, the proprietress and cook, was of commensurable size. Like many first-rate women cooks she had tired eyes and a wan smile. This seemed a happy omen. She said for lunch there would be an omelette with truffles, a *fricandeau* of veal with truffles, asparagus tips, and a local cheese. The little restaurant was of the seventeenth century, the uncovered tables and chairs of the same period. We said it was Shakespearian. So did our friends when they arrived. We were enchanted with the *décor.* Lunch would be worthy of it.

MADAME LOUBET'S ASPARAGUS TIPS

Early spring is the time for the first small green asparagus, very like the wild ones. Wash quickly – do not allow to remain in water – discard white stems. Tie into neat bundles, plunge into boiling salt water. Allow about 8 minutes for their cooking. They should not be over-cooked; much depends upon their freshness. Put aside. Over very low flame put in a saucepan 4 table-spoons butter (for 1 lb. asparagus). When butter is melted, add asparagus tips still tied in bundles. Add 4 tablespoons heavy cream. Do not stir, but gently dip saucepan in all directions until the asparagus are coated with butter and cream. Then remove from flame. Place asparagus on preheated round dish with the points facing to the edge of the dish. Gently cut the strings with kitchen scissors. In the centre place ½ cup heavy whipped cream with ½ teaspoon salt mixed in it. Serve before cream has time to melt. This is a gastronomic feast. And a thing of beauty.

The cheese called Cochat, a speciality of the region, is made of the milk of very young ewes, and ripened in vinegar. It is then pressed under weight and served in the shell of a medium-sized onion. With this it is trad-itional to drink a red wine, preferably a good vintage of Châteauneuf du Pape.

Madame Loubet's cooking was delicate and distin-guished, and we often returned to enjoy it. We could find nothing comparable before the end of our journey. That evening at Marseille a bowl of soup sufficed.

After a long run down the coast of the Mediterranean we arrived at Vence to find a numerous party for dinner. Our friend was something of a *gourmet*, his Belgian cook had a well-organized kitchen and produced varied and succulent menus.

The vegetable garden was already producing spring potatoes, string beans, artichokes, salads, and, before we left, asparagus. The gardener amiably allowed me each morning to gather the day's vegetables. It takes a long time to gather enough very young string beans for eight or ten people. Between the vegetable garden and the rose garden my mornings were happily occupied. To me this pleasure is unequalled.

From Vence we frequently drove down to Nice to have a fish lunch at a small and unpretentious restaurant on the sea. For us they made a local dish –

GRILLED PERCH WITH FENNEL

Wash and completely dry a perch weighing about 3 lb. Rub salt and pepper inside the fish. Paint it with melted butter, paint the grill with butter. Place fish on grill under flame for 25 minutes turning the fish twice and painting it with butter each time. Have a quart of fennel greens washed and dried thoroughly. When the perch is cooked place on a preheated metal dish that withstands flames – not one of pewter, for example. Pour ½ cup melted butter over fish and completely cover with fennel greens. Take to the dining-room, light the fennel leaves. When flaming, serve. It is exciting and delicious, one of the rare Provençal dishes into whose preparation garlic does not enter.

On our trip back to Paris Godiva was no longer inspired. It was we who were obliged to take the initiative. As we were in haste we took no time to go out of the way to discover new places. We contented ourselves with the tried-and-not-found-wanting than which there is nothing more deadly. Once in Paris again she returned to her competent leadership. She took us to Les Andelys where we lunched out of doors at a *bistro* (café-restaurant where coarse but rarely good food is served) on fried fish caught from the Seine just below the terrace where we were lunching. Fish was followed by a really tender Châteaubriand and *soufflé* potatoes. Back in Godiva and on the road again it was obvious that somewhere we had made a wrong turning. Was Godiva or Gertrude Stein at fault? In the discussion that followed we came to no conclusion. We were on the road to Nogent-le-Rotrou. We would see what we would find there. It was an enchanting landscape of thatch-roofed villages, fields coloured with the first poppies and cornflowers and hedges of blossoming hawthorn. Nogent-le-Rotrou was old, clean, and sympathetic. The hotel was furnished with pale Restoration furniture, small figurines and wax flowers under globes were in all the rooms. The food was simple but skilful. We stayed there several days. It was a woman who cooked, quietly and expertly. She showed me how to make

RILLETTES

Grind in meat chopper 2 lb. breast of pork. Melt in iron pot 1 lb. lard. When a pale gold, add chopped pork, 1 tablespoon salt, 1 teaspoon pepper, 1 teaspoon powder for poultry dressing. Simmer uncovered over very low heat for 4 hours, stirring to prevent burning. After

4 hours remove from flame. When cold enough, ladle into jelly glasses. See that meat is evenly distributed. When completely cold, cover with paper. In a cool place the *rillettes* will keep several months. They are nice served with salad or as *hors d'œuvre* or for sandwiches.

On leaving Nogent we took dust roads through the same landscape we had driven through to get there. We were on our way to Senonches, on the edge of a forest. We were seduced at once by the little town, the hotel and the forest. We not only ordered lunch but engaged rooms to spend the night. While waiting for lunch to be cooked, we walked in the forest where Gertrude Stein, who had a good nose for mushrooms, found quantities of them. The cook would be able to tell us if they were edible. Once more a woman was presiding in the kitchen. She smiled when she saw what Gertrude Stein brought for her inspection and pointed to a large basket of them on the kitchen table, but said she would use those Gertrude Stein had found for what she was preparing for our lunch,

A FLAN OF MUSHROOMS À LA CRÈME

Lightly mix 1 cup and 1 tablespoon flour, 4 tablespoons butter, ½ tablespoon salt, and 1 egg. Gently knead this dough on a floured board and roll out. Add 1 tablespoon heavy cream, knead, and roll out. For the third and last time add 1 tablespoon heavy cream, knead, and roll out. Roll into a ball, lightly flour, put in a bowl, cover, and put in a cool place for 1 hour. After an hour's repose, roll out and bake in deep pie plate in preheated oven at 400°. In the meantime prepare

SAUCE MORNAY

Put 2 tablespoons butter in a saucepan over low heat. When melted add 1 medium-sized onion cut in thin slices, 1 medium-sized carrot cut in thin slices, and a stalk of celery cut in thin slices. Turn with a wooden spoon until the vegetables are lightly browned. Add salt and pepper and 1½ tablespoons flour. Turn with a wooden spoon for 5 minutes. Then add slowly 3 cups hot milk. Be careful that there are no lumps. Simmer for ½ hour, stirring frequently to prevent burning. Remove from flame, strain, and discard the vegetables. Add 3 tablespoons heavy cream to strained sauce and ½ cup grated Parmesan cheese. Wash and brush carefully but do not peel 1 lb. small mushrooms. Drain well and wipe dry. Melt 1 tablespoon butter in saucepan, add juice of ½ lemon and 1 tablespoon sherry, salt and a pinch of pepper, paprika, the mushrooms, and ½ clove of mashed garlic. Cover and cook over low flame for 8 minutes. With a perforated spoon remove mushrooms and mix with Mornay sauce. Pour into baked piecrust and place in preheated 450° oven for 12 minutes. Becareful the bottom of the crust does not burn – an asbestos mat under the pie is a protection.

This is a dish that every experienced cook in France prepares in his own way. If morels (edible fungi) are used the cheese is omitted from the sauce. A tomato sauce may be substituted for the Mornay sauce but is not as fine. Chopped ham may be added to the sauce or 4 or 5 boned and crushed anchovies. The variations are endless. The crusts vary too from a biscuit dough to a puff paste. It is a dish that is always well received.

During the winter two of our friends, Janet Scudder the sculptress and Camille Sigard of the Metropolitan Opera of its great days, suggested that they too buy a two-seater Ford and that in summer we should all go south. Janet was hunting a home, the house of her dreams. She was an admirable travelling companion and had a gift for locating good food and first-class wine. When summer came we started off one sunny day to lunch at a restaurant that Janet knew. It was indeed a good lunch but the view from the balcony where lunch was served was too distracting for the enjoyment of a well-prepared meal. We once stayed in the country with friends who had two young sons. At table they chattered to each other continuously but so quietly as not to interfere with our conversation. One day, sitting next to one of them who was silent, I asked why he was not talking to his brother. He explained that he never did when there were artichokes with sauce Mousseline.

Janet in her search for a house would uncover a small *bistro*, but the food was not coarse at the ones Janet took us to. It became a joke whether she and not Godiva had the instinct for achieving the gastronomic bull's-eye. We were on dust roads all the way to Avignon. Maybe we helped, but Godiva led the way to Aramon, a village dominated by a fortified castle, where we lunched roughly but tastily on a dish of the region,

HEN À LA PROVENÇALE

Take a not too old hen and cut into joints, 1 lb. breast or shoulder of mutton, 3 tomatoes, 3 hearts of artichokes, 3 small vegetable marrows, 3 sweet peppers, 1 cup chick peas that have been previously soaked, 3 turnips, 3 medium-sized onions with a clove stuck in each one, 1 teaspoon Spanish red pepper, ¼ teaspoon cumin powder, salt, and a pinch of cayenne. Put in a pot, cover with water, place over medium flame covered. When it boils reduce to low flame and simmer for 2 hours. Serve in a deep dish with chicken and mutton in centre, the vegetables around. Pour as much of the juice as the dish will hold, the rest in a sauceboat. This is not only nourishing and succulent but sufficiently satisfying, with cheese and coffee to follow, to make a meal.

Our friends not yet having found a home were ready to try the Côte d'Azur, expecting us to go too. But neither Gertrude Stein nor I found the Mediterranean coast sympathetic. The part of France that had seduced us by its beauty lay between Avignon and Aix-en-Provence, Orange and the sea. Saint-Rémy would be a point from which to radiate. Janet asked if we had ever eaten there. We were obliged to answer that we had not. We would find out. We had not selected it for its culinary possibilities. Saint-Rémy and the country about had a poignant beauty that would compensate for any material short-comings. At the inn the rough bare rooms they showed us and which I bespoke at once looked out on a pleasant garden. Lunch was ordinary. Janet ominously remarked that we would regret our choice. In the afternoon our friends drove over to Aix-en-Provence and we settled down for a long stay. We were where we wanted to be.

The *mistral* blew and the food was ordinary, but we were enchanted with our walks and drives in all directions. We commenced to look for a passable restaurant or *bistro*. After investigating the provision shops we concluded it was not reasonable to suppose that it could be a country of good cooking. This did not discourage us, it was just a fact. Marseille was within easy reach and we could run down there for diversion, shopping, and a good lunch.

We had had no news from the friends at Aix-en-Provence except a telephone message asking how we were supporting life at Saint-Rémy, when a telegram from Janet announced that we should come over at once to see the house she had found and was busy buying. We drove over next morning. The commonplace little house was built in a hollow – therefore without a view – in a large tract of treeless uncultivated land. Because it was unlike the taste of our friend we tried to dissuade her from buying it, but it had become a fixed idea. We were obliged at lunch to listen endlessly to Janet and her new home. Soon we were going over to see the interior decorations under way and what had been achieved in the well-planned garden.

During this time we had gone down to Marseille and

had tried at two of its best restaurants Marseille's unique creation,

BOUILLABAISSE

The fish should be more than fresh, it should be caught and cooked the same day. This is what gives the dish its quality. There must be many different kinds of fish to give the proper flavour. It is not only the ingredients that go into the sauce – which is not a sauce but a soup – it is the flavour of the fish that predominates. There should be at least five different kinds of fish. In Marseille where the *bouillabaisse* was born there are frequently seven or more not counting the shellfish. It cannot be repeated too often that they must be very fresh. In France there are three different kinds of *bouillabaisse* – the unique and authentic one of Marseille with Mediterranean fish, the one of Paris made of fish from the Atlantic, and a very false one indeed made of fresh-water fish.

Take 5 lb. gurnards, red snapper, red fish, mullets, pike, turbot, and dory, wash, scale, cut off the fins and heads. Cut the large fish in 1-inch slices, leave the smaller ones whole. Have two extra heads of any large fish. Wash very thoroughly and put them with the heads of the small fish with 1 carrot, 1 onion, 1 laurel leaf, a twig of thyme. Cover with 7 cups cold salted water, bring to a boil uncovered. Skim and cover, boil until reduced to half. Then mash with potato masher through fine sieve. Boil 1 large lobster and 1 crab. When cooked remove from water and drain. Cut the meat from the body of the lobster into four pieces. Put the meat from the crab and from all the claws together. Pour into a large saucepan ¼ cup olive oil. When it is hot add ¾ cup thinly sliced onions, 3 crushed shallots, 3 cloves of crushed garlic, ½ sweet pepper (seeds removed), 1 large peeled tomato cut in slices, 4 stalks of celery, 1 two-inch slice of fennel. Turn with a wooden spoon until well coated with oil, then add ¼ cup olive oil, 3 twigs of thyme, 1 laurel leaf, 2 whole cloves, 1 piece of the zest of an orange, salt, and pepper. Over very high heat add the *bouillon* of the fish heads. Boil covered for 5 minutes. Put the less quickly cooked fish into the saucepan. Boil furiously uncovered for 5 minutes. Add the rest of the fish and the lobster meat from the body. Boil furiously uncovered for 5 minutes. Remove from heat. Remove fish and lobster with perforated spoon, wipe whatever may be adhering to them. Place in a large deep dish and keep hot. Strain juice from saucepan, replace on stove, add crab meat and meat from clams. Put in a bowl ¼ teaspoon powdered saffron, mix with 5 tablespoons boiling juice from the saucepan. Mix thoroughly and add to boiling juice. Put around the fish ½-inch slices of French bread. Pour over fish. Serve piping hot.

Very simple *hors d'œuvre* to precede the *Bouillabaisse* – neither vegetable nor fruit juice, please – but raw baby artichokes, endives washed and cut in half, radishes, and asparagus tips for example; with coffee to end a perfect lunch.

We went to Marseille to spend the day two or three times a month and had a *bouillabaisse* at the best of restaurants. We stayed on at Saint-Rémy; summer was over, autumn was even more beautiful. If the *mistral* howled it not only made the sky bluer but all the landscape more vivid. One day we walked to a small Gothic chapel. In a bare field there was a single very large leafless and symmetrical Japanese persimmon tree heavily laden with its deep-orange fruit, silhouetted against the brilliant sky. It remains one of the loveliest of memories.

All day and all night we heard the sheep bells as the flocks were driven into the hills for the winter grazing. We were obliged to take the small roads. The flocks made an effective barrier on the main ones. Janet comfortably installed in her home could not understand why we didn't find Saint-Rémy thoroughly insupportable. The food at the inn even for the Christmas and New Year's celebrations was uninspired. The only thing the little town produced, and that was first rate, was *glacé* fruit, but one could not live upon that alone. French *glacé* fruit differs from our crystallized kind. In France the syrup in which the fruit is cooked is not boiled long enough to crystallize it. In Saint-Rémy there was a manufactory – if anything as unpretentious and small could be called that – of these fruits. They made a speciality of whole *glacé* melons filled with the smaller fruits, cherries, apricots, plums, and pears, delicious and attractive. They sent them to us in Paris until the outbreak of this last war. Like so many other good things, they disappeared with the catastrophe.

As winter wore on, we became restless. Perhaps it was too much *mistral*. It was foolish to leave before the spring came. One day in March, walking through a ploughed field, we were forced to admit that the climate was no longer bearable and that it would be best to leave at once. We took several days to have a last long look at all the places we so little wished to leave and then drove back to Paris.

It had become our habit to remain in Paris during the winter and only take short trips in spring, which however did not prevent us from discussing projects for the long summer vacations. At this time a series of booklets on the gastronomic points of interest in the various regions of France were being published. As each one appeared I would read it with curiosity. The author was paradoxically a professional *gourmet*. Of the places we knew I was not always in agreement with his judgement. However, when it became time to plan the route we were to take to meet the Picassos at Antibes we chose one based on the recommendations of the guides. The first of them was Bourg-en-Bresse.

In May we started off for Chablis, where we would find not only incomparable food but my favourite wine, Chablis. Monsieur Bergeran was an intelligent and gifted *chef*. His menus were a history of the French kitchen and he was its encyclopaedia. One day he said to us that a true *chef* should have no secrets, that anyone could know everything there was to know about cooking. There should be no tricks or secrets. To prove this he asked me to come and see him at work. This is the way I saw him prepare

CHICKEN SAUTÉ AUX DUCS DE BOURGOGNE

Cut a fine roasting chicken into six pieces. Brown them in 4 tablespoons butter over medium flame in Dutch oven. When browned add salt and pepper, cover and put in preheated 350° oven. Baste frequently and turn once. It will take between ¾ hour to 1 hour to cook according to size of chicken. When the chicken is cooked remove from flame and place the pieces of chicken on preheated carving dish. Put the Dutch oven over medium flame and add ¾ cup port, ½ cup brandy, ¼ cup whisky, and ¼ cup best kirsch. Detach from oven with spatula any glaze that may be adhering to it. Mix well. In a bowl stir 2 yolks of eggs and slowly add 2 cups warm cream. Pour slowly into Dutch oven. Heat thoroughly but do not allow to boil. Tip in all directions. Do not stir. Pour over chicken and serve hot.

From Chablis we went to Dijon, where we had for dinner at the famous restaurant of the Three Pheasants

SUPRÈME OF PIKE À LA DIJONAISE

Cut the fillets from a pike, see that no bones adhere, and then skin them. Interlard them as one does fillet of beef. Put them in a deep dish with ¼ cup brandy, ½ cup sherry, and 1 cup good dry red wine, salt and pepper and 4 shallots chopped fine and 4 bouquets each containing 1 stalk of celery, 1 small twig of thyme, and ¼ laurel leaf, each bouquet tied in a muslin bag. Baste with liquid and put aside. In winter keep for 48 hours, in summer for 24 hours, basting twice a day. When the fillets are ready to be cooked place in a deep earthenware dish which has been heavily coated with soft butter, the fillets, the four little bags, and the strained marinade. Put into preheated oven 400° for about 20 minutes, basting frequently. When the fillets are well browned, remove from oven, add 2 tablespoons cream and 3 tablespoons soft butter. Baste and serve at once.

From Dijon our road led to Bourg-en-Bresse, recommended by the *Guide Gastronomique*, through the country renowned for its chickens of the large and thick breasts and short legs. Bourg is a well-known market town, not only for its fowl but for dairy produce and vegetables. We fell under its spell at once. The menu at the hotel for dinner was carefully chosen and delicately cooked. We were delighted and toasted the guide book which had led us there and decided to stay for a couple of days. In the morning we visited the market and the provision shops, regretting that we did not live in the region – not suspecting that we were to spend six months a year for seventeen consecutive years within twenty-five miles of it. For lunch we had

TURNOVERS WITH CRAWFISH – SAUCE NANTUA

Make a puff paste, roll in a ball, and put aside in a cool place. Dice 2 medium-sized carrots, 2 medium-sized onions, cut 1 stalk of celery in rings. Put 2 tablespoons butter in saucepan and when melted brown the vegetables in it. When browned, put into the saucepan 1 cup dry white wine and 48 unshelled crawfish. Cover and cook over medium heat for 10 minutes. Remove the crawfish with a perforated spoon. Remove their shells.

Put the crawfish aside, and the shells and the diced vegetables into a mortar and pound until fine enough to strain through a fine sieve. Add 1 cup thick cream sauce, the strained juice in which the crawfish have cooked, 2 tablespoons soft butter, 1 teaspoon cognac. Mix well and cool. Roll out the puffpaste ¼ inch thick. Cut in squares of 4 inches and put 4 crawfish towards one corner with 1 tablespoon sauce which must be cold. Turn the opposite corner over to cover the crawfish. Press around the edges firmly with the floured handle of a small knife. Paint lightly with a stirred egg and put on lightly buttered baking sheet and bake in preheated oven 400° for 20 minutes. While the turnovers are baking keep the rest of the sauce hot. When the turnovers are baked remove from oven and place on preheated plate, and pour some of the sauce on each one of them.

These turnovers are very popular in the Bresse and the Bugey for Sunday lunch, for baptisms, and for weddings.

From the same source the advice that had taken us to Bourg took us to Belley. The short ride was through a pleasing country. Belley was a small town on a hillside with varied landscape on all sides. For our evening meal we ordered simply a poached fish with brown butter, a vegetable salad, and raspberries, it was satisfactory. We took a walk round the outside of the town and were enchanted. Though not actually in the mountains Belley had mountain air from the not far distant Alps. The next morning early we drove in Godiva in all directions. The country was beautiful and diversified. The people on the roads and in the fields were upstanding and had an air of well being. The children were charmingly pretty. In the hills there were lakes and in the valleys there were streams. It was too good to be true. We got back to the hotel for lunch. It was only then that we remembered how enthusiastically the cooking at the hotel had been recommended. The menu was a stock one, the cooking unadventurous. Even so we would stay on to see more of the country. We wired to the Picassos that we were delayed, we would get to them within a week. The proprietress of the hotel – her husband was the cook who preferred reading Lamartine in a corner to doing his work in the kitchen – when she heard we were staying on moved us to larger rooms with a view over a garden with the hills in the background.

Everything had been so much to our taste that we had been indifferent to the cooking. It was workaday and would probably not change. For the moment at least this was of no importance. At the end of the week when we drove over to Aix-les-Bains and had an unpretentious well-cooked lunch at a restaurant by the lakeside we could laugh at the cooking of the hotel at Belley.

Gertrude Stein wrote to Picasso that we were not going south this year, we found Belley sympathetic and were spending the summer there.

One evening a beautiful woman sat at the little table next to us, her book turned towards us. After several days she suddenly asked, half turning her head, if we had Lavaret for dinner every night, to which we answered that we did. Several evenings later in the same fashion she asked why we had Lavaret every evening for dinner. Gertrude Stein told her that it was the most carefully prepared dish on the menu. Obviously, said the lady. One day we met her in the street and we stopped to talk. She told us of several restaurants in small towns, even in villages, in the region where we could eat extremely well. Godiva took us to all of them. We had not after all lost our taste for food. We went to the Haute Savoie and on the lake of Annecy had remarkably good lunches, to Artemarre which pleased us even more, and to Saint-Genix where in a simple *décor* we enjoyed uncommonly good cooking. But our favourite restaurant was totally unlike these, both for its quality and its simplicity. It had been a *bistro* before Madame Bourgeois for family reasons had taken it over. Within a short time it had become known by French *gourmets* as one of the best restaurants in France. Madame Bourgeois was a perfect cook. To the simplest dishes was given as much attention as to the most complicated, which occasionally included the great dishes created in the last three centuries. We drove over often to Priay, a village of 341 inhabitants near the river Ain which is known for its superior fish, in a hunting district abounding in pheasants, partridges, and grouse, and within easy driving distance of the great markets of Lyon. Monsieur Bourgeois was a great judge of wine and went each autumn to the annual auction at the Hospice at Beaune, returning with its best. We got to know the Bourgeois very well and always spent a moment with them in the kitchen, which was thoroughly organized and equipped and very nearly noiseless. From Madame Bourgeois I learned much of what great French cooking was and had been, but because she was a genius in her way, I did not learn from her any one single dish. The inspiration of genius is neither learned nor taught.

After the vintage it had turned cold and we went back to Paris. By April we had returned to Belley to the same pleasant hotel and its poor food. Friends came to stay with us and we would drive them to lunch at Aix-les-Bains, Artemarre, and Annecy, but above all to Priay.

Before the end of the summer we realized that we must either build, buy, or rent a house somewhere in the country near Belley. But that was a large order. We spent two summers at it. The land we wanted to buy was either not for sale or had no water, the houses were not for sale or had little water. There were no houses to rent that we would have moved into. We were miserable until one afternoon we glimpsed the perfect house from across the valley. It was neither for sale nor to rent but this time nothing would prevent our securing the summer home of our dreams. It was let to an officer in garrison at Belley. How did one dislodge a tenant without a legal reason? We talked to the owner of the house who plainly showed he considered us quite mad, but he told us that his tenant was a captain, and that there were too many majors in the battalion. That was enough to inspire us. We would get two influential friends in Paris to have him promoted, he would be ordered to another garrison, and the house would be free for us. Soon after our return to Paris the captain came up to Versailles to take his examinations. He failed to pass them. Our friends said we were not to worry, in three months he had the right to try again. And once more he failed. We were despondent. Someone suggested his being appointed to Africa, at advanced pay and tantamount to promotion. The captain accepted, the friends became active again and soon we were ecstatically tenants of a house which we had never seen nearer than two miles away.

Godiva was tired and old and Gertrude Stein in spring bought a new car and we drove down to Bilignin in it with a white poodle pup to find the house better than our dreams of it.

HASCHICH FUDGE

(which anyone could whip up on a rainy day)

This is the food of Paradise – of Baudelaire's Artificial Paradises: it might provide an entertaining refreshment for a Ladies' Bridge Club or a chapter meeting of the DAR. In Morocco it is thought to be good for warding off the common cold in damp winter weather and is, indeed, more effective if taken with large quantities of hot mint tea. Euphoria and brilliant storms of laughter, ecstatic reveries and extensions of one's personality on several simultaneous planes are to be complacently expected. Almost anything Saint Teresa did, you can do better if you can bear to be ravished by *un évanouissement réveillé*.

Take 1 teaspoon black peppercorns, 1 whole nutmeg, 4 average sticks of cinnamon, 1 teaspoon coriander. These should all be pulverized in a mortar. About a handful each of stoned dates, dried figs, shelled almonds, and peanuts: chop these and mix them together. A bunch of *canibus sativa* can be pulverized. This along with the spices should be dusted over the mixed fruit and nuts, kneaded together. About a cup of sugar dissolved in a big pat of butter. Rolled into a cake and cut into pieces or made into balls about the size of a walnut, it should be eaten with care. Two pieces are quite sufficient.

Obtaining the *canibus* may present certain difficulties, but the variety known as *canibus sativa* grows as a common weed, often unrecognized, everywhere in Europe, Asia, and parts of Africa; besides being cultivated as a crop for the manufacture of rope. In the Americas, while often discouraged, its cousin, called *canibus indica*, has been observed even in city window boxes. It should be picked and dried as soon as it has gone to seed and while the plant is still green.

······ GREAT   FOOD ······

RECIPES AND LESSONS FROM A DELICIOUS COOKING REVOLUTION

Alice Waters

A CHAMPION OF ORGANIC, locally produced and seasonal food and founder of acclaimed Californian restaurant Chez Panisse, Alice Waters has recently been awarded the *Légion d'honneur* in France for her contributions to food culture. In this book, she explores the simplest of dishes in the most delicious of ways, with fresh, sustainable ingredients a must, even encouraging cooks to plant their own garden.

From orange and olive salad to lemon curd and ginger snaps, Waters constantly emphasizes the joys and ease of cooking with local, fresh food, whether in soups, salads or sensual, classic desserts.

'Waters is a legend'
JAY RAYNER

GREAT FOOD

FROM ABSINTHE TO ZEST
An Alphabet for Food Lovers

Alexandre Dumas

AS WELL AS BEING THE AUTHOR OF *The Three Musketeers*, Alexandre Dumas was also an enthusiastic gourmand and expert cook. His *Grand Dictionnaire de Cuisine*, published in 1873, is an encyclopaedic collection of ingredients, recipes and anecdotes, from Absinthe to Zest via cake, frogs' legs, oysters, roquefort and vanilla.

Included here are recipes for bamboo pickle and strawberry omelette, advice on cooking all manner of beast from bear to kangaroo – as well as delightful digressions into how a fig started a war and whether truffles really increase ardour – brought together in a witty and gloriously eccentric culinary compendium.

'From the great French novelist and obsessive gourmet. The cook book as literature'
NORMAN SPINRAD

GREAT  FOOD

THE PLEASURES OF THE TABLE
Jean-Anthelme Brillat-Savarin

EPICURE AND GOURMAND Brillat-Savarin was one of the most influential food writers of all time. His 1825 book *The Physiology of Taste* defined our notions of French gastronomy, and his insistence that food be a civilizing pleasure for all has inspired the slow food movement and guided chefs worldwide.

From discourses on the erotic properties of truffles and the origins of chocolate, to a defence of gourmandism and why 'a dessert without cheese is like a pretty woman with only one eye', the delightful writings in this selection are a hymn to the art of eating well.

*'Marvellously tart and smart, and also
comfortingly, absurdly French'*
AA GILL

GREAT FOOD

A TASTE OF THE SUN

Elizabeth David

LEGENDARY COOK AND WRITER Elizabeth David
changed the way Britain ate, introducing a postwar nation
to the sun-drenched delights of the Mediterranean, and
bringing new flavours and aromas such as garlic,
wine and olive oil into its kitchens.

This mouthwatering selection of her writings and
recipes embraces the richness of French and Italian cuisine,
from earthy cassoulets to the simplest spaghetti, as well as
evoking the smell of buttered toast, the colours of foreign
markets and the pleasures of picnics. Rich with anecdote,
David's writing is defined by a passion for good, authentic,
well-balanced food that still inspires chefs today.

*'Above all, Elizabeth David's books
make you want to cook'*
TERENCE CONRAN

GREAT FOOD

A LITTLE DINNER BEFORE THE PLAY

Agnes Jekyll

WHETHER EXTOLLING THE MERITS of a cheerful breakfast tray, conjuring up a winter picnic of figs and mulled wine, sharing delicious Tuscan recipes, or suggesting a last-minute pre-theatre dinner, the sparkling writings of the society hostess and philanthropist Agnes Jekyll describe food for every imaginable occasion and mood.

Originally published in *The Times* in the early 1920s, these divinely witty and brilliantly observed pieces are still loved today for their warmth and friendly advice and, with their emphasis on fresh, simple, stylish dishes, were years ahead of their time.

'Beautifully written, sparkling, witty and knowing, an absolute delight to read'
INDIA KNIGHT

GREAT FOOD

A MIDDLE EASTERN FEAST
Claudia Roden

AWARD-WINNING FOOD WRITER Claudia Roden
revolutionized Western attitudes to the cuisines of the
Middle East with her bestselling *Book of Middle Eastern
Food*. Introducing millions to enticing new scents and
flavours, her intensely personal, passionate writings
conveyed an age-old tradition of family eating and shared
memory. This selection includes recipes for tagines from
Morocco, rice from Iran, peasant soup from ancient
Egypt and kofta from Armenia, as well as discussions of
spices, market bargaining, childhood memories of Cairo
and the etiquette of tea drinking; evoking not only a
cuisine but an entire way of life.

*'Roden's great gift is to conjure up not just a cuisine
but the culture from which it springs'*
NIGELLA LAWSON

GREAT FOOD

EXCITING FOOD FOR SOUTHERN TYPES

Pellegrino Artusi

PELLEGRINO ARTUSI is the original icon of
Italian cookery, whose legendary 1891 book *Science
in the Kitchen and the Art of Eating Well* defined its
national cuisine and is still a bestseller today.

He was also a passionate gastronome, renowned
host and brilliant raconteur, who filled his books with
tasty recipes and rumbustious anecdotes. From an
unfortunate incident regarding minestrone in Livorno
and a proud defence of the humble meat loaf, to
digressions on the unusual history of ice-cream, the
side-effects of cabbage and the Florentines' weak
constitutions, these writings brim with gossip, good
cheer and an inexhaustible zest for life.

'The fountainhead of modern Italian cookery'
GASTRONOMICA

GREAT FOOD

THROUGHOUT the history of civilization, food has been
livelihood, status symbol, entertainment — and passion.
The twenty fine food writers here, reflecting on different
cuisines from across the centuries and around the globe, have
influenced each other and continue to influence us today,
opening the door to the wonders of every kitchen.